Our Hoosier Heritage and Its Foundation
1680-1820

Why We Are Called Hoosiers

Ron Bell

M. T. Publishing Company, Inc. ™

P.O. Box 6802
Evansville, Indiana 47719-6802
www.mtpublishing.com

Library of Congress Control Number: 2015959839

ISBN: 978-1-938730-85-6

Graphic Designer: Thalita A. Floyd-Wingerter

Printed in the United States of America

Comments

As a youth growing up in Indiana, I never saw an "Indian" in Indiana and was unaware of what tribes were the reason our state was given such a name. I was aware that flint and stone tools were commonly found on local streams and farms. But when talking to those finders and asking what Indians they were from, they normally were as dumbfounded as I. In talking to persons who claimed Indian heritage in their families, many did not know what tribe their heritage came from. In compliance with the early settlers' feelings that "the only good Indian was a dead Indian," the great-great grandchildren of those Indians who are still in this area seem to feel that the best Indian history is the forgotten Indian history. I think all of Indiana deserves a better recollection of the tumultuous and exciting days when white settlers and the Indians were challenging each other for the dominant society in our area.

One problem with trying to make sense out of this history is that the stage on which it was set was a very large one. It extended from Pittsburgh on the east to St. Louis on the west. From northern Michigan to southern Kentucky. It was played out from the 1500's through 1838. By historical standards, there were only a few actors at any one time—a couple of hundred key actors on each side with possible two thousand extras. History could have been decisively turned in different ways by any of the sides with a thousand competent, battle-experienced men. The bravado of individuals on both sides is almost legendary. The atrocities committed on the Midwestern stage, if understood in complete detail, would turn the stomach. Only brief hints can be found in history since it was accomplished and observed by woods-trained people, not book-learned scholars. But the fact of the events is that their conflict did change the course of history. The lands north of the Ohio could have been part of Canada and mainly a red man's nation. Indiana today could have been woods and wildlife, not farms and commerce, with trails and canoes, not four-lane highways and eighteen-wheel trucks. The lands west of the Appalachians might have been withdrawn from the colonies to become a separate nation with its trade route based on the Mississippi River.

This area could be compared to a large chess board. However, the board was never cleared of a previous game when a new one started. The first game was played with various shades of red pawns. They played with a vengeance and reduced the numbers of pawns to only a few left on the board when a new game started. The new one was between the English and the French. They started with only a few players on the board but added pawns when they could. There were only a few bishops, knights and rooks on the board for either side, and the main pieces, the kings and queens, were never on the board at any time in any contest. The choice pieces were in Europe or on the east coast of America. The object of the game was never to capture the main piece and complete the contest. It was played to determine the rules of the game on the playing field—a minor item for the "kings and queens," but a major consideration for the pawns.

The game was played to determine what the rules of the game would be. Would it be a hunting and subsistence culture based on loose local control? Would it be a feeder colony to send raw materials to the foreign "king"? Would the board be controlled by the pawns or by the kings? Who would own the board the game was played on? Would it be the Indians, French, English, Spanish, Americans or a new yet unnamed country headed by a yet unnamed social order?

The game is still being played. The pieces have been transformed into entities that the early pawns would not even recognize. However, the game is still the same. What will be the current rules of the game?

We cannot understand the current game unless we know the history of the game. That knowledge will probably not change the game, but it will at least let us know that we are playing a long term game and not just marking time.

Most of the following narrations are not original—they are historical in spirit. Since I was not there to watch the events reported, I have had to rely on earlier writers who were there or reports that were found in the dark holes of history. Most of early writers' works are now out of print and generally unavaliable. The purpose of this book is to help put a little light on the events of Indiana history and hopefully enlighten curious persons interested in what happened here. While copious use of dates are used in the book's naration, the dates are only meant to give a timeline reference to that event and to other events in the book.

Contents

Chapter 1
The Development of the Land
That Would Later Be Indiana

Many of the early Indian tribes that had lived in the Ohio River Valley were only a memory when the first French explorers came to this area in the 1670's.

One of these tribes, the Capuanos, lived up the Ohio River from Mississippi. They were a Shawnee sub group and in great number. They had 38 villages. In one district were 23 in close geographic location, and 15 villages in another district. At that time the tribes were a peaceful people, far enough away from the Iroquois to not be harassed by the eastern tribes.

Villages above the Falls of the Ohio on the north side of river, from the river forks at Pittsburgh to the west, included the Erie (alias Black Minqua alias Kentaientonga) which had 19 villages, while the Honniasontkeronons (alias Oniassontke) had two villages and the Casa, one village. The Mosapelea lived in eight villages.

In Kentucky and above the Green River were villages of the Casakepe (associated with the western Shawnee) and Meguatchaiki (later the Mekoce division of the Shawnee).

The villages were located at the head of a trade trail that went south to Spanish trade posts. This trail was also used by the Chiouanons (alias Chaouenonsa alias Shawnee) and the Casquinampo Indians. Below the Louisville Falls were the Outagame and Iskousogos.

Above the Louisville Falls were the Honniasontkeronons and Chiouanons. At unknown locations on the Ohio River were the Tougue and Antastoez (Susquehannock subgroup).

Other tribal names mentioned in early records as residing in the greater Ohio River system in the late prehistoric time period, but for which no linguistic or cultural information has been located, include Caskinampu, Kaskinonea, Cisca, Tomahitans, Monetons, Monetans, Massomacks and Arriganagas The Ohio River was called Mosopeleacipi or Olighin by some of the tribes.

A lot of name confusion abounds in this time period because the sources quoted were from various European nations that called each tribe by their own definition of the spelling and pronunciation of tribal words, as well as which tribal language group (Iroquois, Algonquin, or other) the source of the word came from.

With the arrival of the French, the native settlement pattern changed in the lower Northwest Territory. Returning tribes included the Miami and their various sub clans. The Miami tribal family include the Wea and the Piankashaw Indians. The Miami tribe was first encountered by the French in the Wisconsin area before 1679, but were later found at the south end of Lake Michigan in 1680. Lore states that the Miami had been driven into Wisconsin by the Iroquois raids into the Midwest area. After 1680, the main Miami villages were located at the south end of

Lake Michigan, along the upper Wabash River and on the Maumee River in Ohio. They were known to send war parties to the Iroquois in New York, Pennsylvania and Maryland in the 1600 and 1700 time period. They also made peaceful trade overtures to colonials in Virginia in the early 1700's. Late arriving tribes include the Kickapoo and Potawatomi.

As the Europeans encroached on the eastern tribal areas, some tribal groups moved into the area north of the Ohio River. These include the Delaware groups that include the Munsee and Mahican tribes as well as Shawnee groups that had returned from the south. The movement was supervised by the Iroquois federation with the intent of using the permitted Indians to serve as a buffer to the western tribes that had raided the Iroquois homelands.

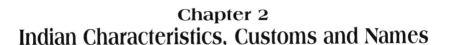

Chapter 2
Indian Characteristics, Customs and Names

In general the Indians seemed to have been taller than the Europeans, averaging 5'8" to 5'10". Their bone structure was finer, their muscles smoother and more graceful. They had slender waists, broad cheekbones and somewhat Roman noses. Often their foreheads were sloped, a deformity caused by the practice of lashing the babies' heads to cradle boards. Body decorations consisted of tattoos and large earrings hung from enlarged and stretched earlobes. The Miami Indians were gentle, affable, and sedate. Their language was in harmony with their dignity. They spoke slowly and maintained great interest in what was told them. Their subgroup of Piankashaws were the most peaceful towards the European settlers. The Potawatomi were duller Indians and their language was more guttural. In 1672, the Wea were in central Wisconsin but had moved into northern Indiana by 1710. Kickapoo Indians (the lightest skinned Indians in the area) were poor fighters in large groups, but excelled in long-range raids into Kentucky, in small groups of five to 20 warriors.

Warder Stevens wrote in his *Centennial History of Washing County, Indiana* that "Among all the Indians there was a striking uniformity in their appearance, character, manners, customs and opinions. As to color they were all of a reddish copper, with some diversity of shade. The men were tall, large-boned and well-made; with small black eyes, lodged in deep sockets, high cheek bones, nose more or less aquiline, mouth large, lips rather thick and the hair of the head black, straight and coarse. They wore no beard, carefully extracting every hair that might make its appearance on the face. At the present time one may be seen sporting a light mustache. Their general expression of countenance was thoughtful and sedate. They were little given to mirth, had sound understanding, quick apprehension, a retentive memory, with an air of indifference in their general behavior. The women, or squaws, differed considerably from the men, both in person and features. They were small and short, with homely broad faces, which often wore expression of mildness and even sweetness.... All spoke in low tones of voice and employed few words in casual conversation, but their chiefs, in council, would become loud, rapid and vehement.

"The sight, smell and hearing of the Indian, being frequently and attentively exercised, were acute. They could trace the footsteps of man or beast through the forest or swamp, when an inexperienced eye could not discern the slightest vestige. They could pursue the course through the pathless forest or over vast plains with undeviating certainty, being guided by marks which would have entirely escaped the notice of the white man. Their distinguishing qualities were strength, cunning and ferocity, and as war was their chief employment, so bravery was their main virtue.

"Their dress differed considerably in different tribes or nations. The Indians found in Indiana were mostly clothed in fur robes and blankets. Everything they could seize upon in the way of gaudy trinkets or ornamentation was rapidly appropriated. Much time was spent by the squaws in fashioning out of furs and feathers the showiest kind of head dress, belts, and neckwear.... Leggings protected the lower limbs and moccasins the feet. A breech cloth, fastened to a girdle, passed around the loins and lower part of the body. In some tribes the hair was allowed to flow loosely over the shoulders. In others it was carefully braided, knotted and ornamented as well as soaked in grease. Most of them suspended from their ears wampum beads and trinkets of various kinds. They were fond of bracelets and rings. Beads of various kinds were the favorite ornament for the squaws, but they took more pride in painting up and adorning their husbands than themselves. The woman who could turn out the most gaudily bedecked warrior was the envy of everyone else. The wigwams or lodges of the Indians were differently constructed in different tribes. The modest were formed of poles stood up against trees or benches of rock, covered with grass or cedar boughs. A more pretentious shelter was made of poles stuck in the ground in a circle, the tops being brought together and tied with pliant strips of bark or vine of some sort. Skins of wild beasts were often used for tent covering, making very comfortable quarters for the winter. Light was admitted by a small doorway, and by an aperture at the top, which also served for the escape of smoke. Fires were kindled in the middle of the lodge, and the family sat around on the bare ground, but skins were spread for a visitor. Indians at the time this country was first settled, learned to start fires with flint and steel from the whites. Cooking utensils were few. In some instances a pot or kettle was procured from white traders, but more often an earthen pot of their own make was the only utensil used around the fire. Wooden bowls were sometimes used in serving meals. The stomach or skull of some animal was used for carrying water and hot stones were used in heating water as necessity demanded. Their food consisted in the main of parched corn, wild fruit, fish and the flesh of wild animals. They had no fixed time for meals, but ate when they were hungry.

"Indians never chastised their children, especially the boys, thinking it would dampen their spirits, check their love of independence and cool their martial ardor. Parents would endeavor to train them in diligence and skill in hunting and inspire them in courage and contempt of danger, pain, or death. When advanced in life and no longer able to participate in the chase or take part in war, they often longed for the hour of death.

"Among the red men, society was always in the loosest state in which it could possibly exist. They had no laws, no magistrates or tribunals to protect the weak or punish the guilty. Every man asserted his own rights and avenged his own wrongs. He was neither restrained nor protected by anything but his innate sense of shame, or the prompting of honor, together with the approbation or disapprobation of his tribe. His misdeeds sometimes caused him to be cut off from his own people, to become a wandering miscreant doomed to an untimely death. Among these people sentiment and habit often did more to curb passion and set matters aright than the wise laws accomplish in civilized society. They were always ambitious to preserve the honor of their tribe or nation, proud of its success, and zealous for its welfare. No people were ever more ready to sacrifice everything, even life itself if necessary, for their tribe. When all were equally poor, the distinction founded on wealth cannot exist and among a people for whom experience is the only source of knowledge, the aged men are naturally the sages of the nation. The chief was merely the most confidential individual in the tribe, and was never installed with a ceremony nor distinguished by any badge. The men of the tribe usually settled their controversies among themselves, seldom applying to the chief except for advice."

While most Indian names are not easily pronounced in English, it has been assumed that the American version of the Indian name was made up by whites dealing with the Indian. Normally that was not true. The name usually was a literal translation of the Indian version of that name. However, an Indian might change his name at various times in his life if the tribal council thought it could describe him better with a new name.

The name of an Indian boy was not given casually by his parents at his birth. As a small child, he was a nameless boy. Usually his name was given to him by a tribal council when he became of age. The name was based on physical excellence, physical peculiarity, prowess in war, or a distinguishing feature of the individual in the tribe. There was a preponderance of names like "Big Bear," "Iron Horn Bull," "Fast Horse," "Little Bull," "Big Bull," "Wolf," "Panther" and "Mountain Lion."

Physical peculiarities were indicated by names as well: "Big Thigh," "Poor Shoulder Blade," "Walks Like a Boy," "Hawk Traces," "Wrinkle Face," "Red All Over," "Left Hand," "Squint Eyes," "One Eye," "No Eyes," "Iron Voice" and "Woman's Hip."

Confirmed habits and disposition were indicated by such names as "Shaved Clean," "Dirty Ear," "Strikes his Breast," "Steals Tobacco," "Beats His Wife," "Lying White Man," "Kicking Woman," "Cold Feet," "Chief Coward," "Steals Gun at Night," "Man Who Steals Woman" and "Man Loves Tobacco."

Exploits and physical prowess are shown in names like "Big Brave," "Strangled the Wolf," "Chief on the Prairie," "Chief All Over," "Good Stabber," "Ready to Shoot," "Man Who Don't Run," "Fight Like Bear," "Take It Alive" and "Many Wounds."

Some names were given in derision or contempt such as "Stays In Camp," "Grandmother," "Temporarily Married," "Lots of Sleep," "Squaw Beater," "Takes Back Gifts" and "Yellow Liver."

Some idea of worldly goods is indicated by some names such as "Twelve Blankets," "Heavy Gun," "Two Guns," "Many Horses," "Plenty of Fat" and "Tall Hat."

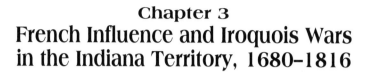

Chapter 3
French Influence and Iroquois Wars in the Indiana Territory, 1680–1816

In the time before contact with the Europeans, the Iroquois claimed land title to the Ohio River Valley, the Northwest Territory and Kentucky, by right of conquest over a several hundred year time period. One newspaper story found in New Albany referred to a colony of Aztecs at the Falls of the Ohio area who were massacred around the time of Cortez's invasion of Mexico (1519). They had been recalled to help defend their Aztec homeland. They were getting ready to depart down what was later known as the Natchez Trail when a hostile Indian group attacked and killed the Aztec and the local Indian tribe before the Aztecs could depart.

The Iroquois had no major village settlements in this area but used it as a hunting ground. Other Indian groups violated the area at will and challenged the Iroquois possession. The risk of retaliation by the Iroquois federation led to several wars and annihilation of many western tribes before European settlers came to this area. The first written reference in French correspondence, found in 1634, said the Miami and other tribes had been driven away from the main peninsula of Michigan by the Iroquois to west of Lake Michigan into the Wisconsin area. The letter said that Michigan had become a "no man's land." It is inferred that the same fate had occurred to Ohio, Indiana and Kentucky territories areas as well. The Iroquois had firearms given to them by the English and Dutch. The Miami did not. The purpose of this Iroquois raid was to allow the Iroquois to become the middlemen in the western fur trade for the English.

The destruction of the Ohio River Valley tribes by Eastern tribes ended about 1700, but the Beaver Wars and the French and Indian War gave claim to both the British and French to territorial rights in the Ohio River Valley. Both had sponsored raids into that area before 1760's.

The New York Iroquois name for the western Indians were *Far Indians*, *Naked Indians*, *Lakes Indians* and *Mingoes*.

Robert Rene Cavalier Sieur de LaSalle's first expedition began in 1669. His expedition from Hamilton, Ontario, eventually reached the Ohio River and followed the river as far as the falls at the later location of Louisville, Kentucky.

LaSalle continued to explore the upper Midwest and in 1680. La Salle and his crew followed the Miami River to South Bend, Indiana, where it joins the Kankakee River.

In 1681, LaSalle sponsored a council meeting hosted by the Miami Indians. The purpose of the council was for LaSalle to encourage the Indians to form a mutual protection treaty against the Iroquois. His message was that separately each tribe would be at the mercy of the Iroquois and be beaten. Together they could defend the territory against the invasion. The Indians agreed and formalized the treaty in May 1681 at the Council Oak, in Highland Cemetery, South Bend, Indiana. The treaty meeting was called because in 1680 an expedition of Iroquois Indians came into the Illinois Territory from New York and fought with the Potawatomi, Fox and other tribes in upper Illinois.

Upon returning to Indiana Territory from Illinois, the Iroquois were met by the local Miami Indians, who had laid an ambush for them near Terre Haute's future location. The Miami were beaten by the Iroquois at what the Indians called the "Old Battle Ground." The Iroquois took several hundred Indian prisoners back to New York with them from the Midwest. They cooked and ate about half of their captives.

LaSalle had been warned that other French, English and Dutch traders were against his exploration of the west. They tried to have him assassinated by men in his employ and tried to poison his food on several occasions. LaSalle was also warned that if the other trade interests could not stop him, they would arouse the Iroquois Indians against the tribes he traded with. One of the priests with LaSalle, Father Louis Hennepin, stated in his writings that "the Iroquois had killed more than two million of the people in that vast extended country." They had not only killed whole villages, but whole tribes. Credence can be given to these comments by the fact that around 1780, the Indians showed George Rogers Clark the scattered bones of hundreds of people killed and left to lay where they dropped on the islands downriver from the Falls of the Ohio and near the later site of New Albany, Indiana. That island is now called Sand Island.

The Miami had formerly lived beyond the Mississippi, but had migrated eastward through Wisconsin and northern Illinois and around Lake Michigan to Detroit. They were part of a larger Illinois Indian nation which included the Fox, Sac, Muscatine and Kickapoo. Although distant blood relatives, these tribes fought readily with each other before Europeans come into the area. The causes of the conflict were ancient and complex. Each death of an Indian in a war called for his kin to return the deed for the good of the tribe's reputation and the soul of the departed. Some tribes that had been great a century earlier were reduced to small bands of less than a hundred by the time the French arrived. War was their intramural sport and the "score" was kept in the number of lives in the tribe. Being a docile or submissive tribe or tribal member at this time was not an asset to self or community. By 1700, the Indians of the Miami, Eel River, Ouiatanon, Piankashaw and other smaller tribes started to settle or resettle within the boundaries of Indiana. Earlier they were afraid to live in Indiana because of their fear of the Iroquois, but now they had firearms. The Iroquois returned and were roughly handled by the Miami, on what was now equal terms, at a location north of Terre Haute near where Fort Harrison was later built. The Iroquois engaged the combined forces of the Illinois and Miami Indians. The Iroquois were attacked on both sides of the Wabash River at that point. The battle lasted for three days and nights. The Iroquois were never a threat to the Indians of Illinois or Indiana territory again.

When George Rogers Clark wanted to settle north of the Ohio River, the Indians could not understand why anyone would want to settle there because of the "*bad history and bad spirits of the land.*" Because of that history, many Indians referred to the Ohio River as the "Dark and Bloody River."

Chapter 4
Early Native Contact with the French and English, 1690-1790

The French King Louis XIV revoked the license of his fur traders serving the western tribal villages of the Miami, Wea and Fox. He desired to cause the Indians to trade at approved trading posts that were also manned with French military troops. It is thought that Post Miami (Fort Wayne) was started in 1697 as one of the King's main trading posts. This location was near the Indian village of Kekionga. This village served as the capital of the Miami nation and its several associated tribes.

In the 1690's, great caravans of pack horses left Charlestown and Savannah in quest of deer skins, fur and young Indian slaves. The trade was so successful that the yearly export of deer skins to London was 54,000 from the southeastern parts of North America. Some of these trains are thought to have made intrusion into the Ohio and White River valleys. These traders may have been using a then-secret passage through the mountains, now known as the Cumberland Gap. The Indian slaves when sold were used to cut timber, saw lumber, tend to burning tar kilns and collect rosin, or were sold to buyers in the West Indies and New England. The rowdy trappers and traders from Charlestown were blazing the trails with which their grandchildren would flood Kentucky and the Northwest Territory seventy years later. In its earliest days, the trail was kept a secret by the few European traders who knew of its existence. At this time there were only about 200 traders working out of Charlestown. How many made it into the Ohio River Valley is not known. Many of them stood in jeopardy of the law when they appeared at the spring rendezvous in Charlestown. The only scruples they showed was the prudence of not offending powerful tribes which might seek vengeful retaliations.

In the 1700's, the Indian villages became a two-party trading group, some trading with the French and some with the English. French partisans in the paint and feathers of warriors led savages in long expeditions against the English on the frontier. Of the five nations living in primarily four villages, there were sixty men with firearms and a combined force of six to seven hundred warriors. The Spanish, west of the Mississippi, were also trading for fur east of the Mississippi River into the Wabash Valley. Their total trade take is not known.

The Indians tribes were in close proximity to the French forts in the 1700's for protection from hostile tribes and the English. Piankashaw Indian villages along the east fork of White River, referred to as "old Indian villages" on early maps, were abandoned for northern Indiana villages at the encouragement of the French. The French thought the east fork of White River was an easy area for the Indians to trade with the English traders and away from the French control.

By 1702, "the Carolina traders were boldly floating down the Ohio River to meet voyageurs from Illinois, who were not above selling their peltries to the enemy. In fact some Frenchmen traveled to British held territory knowing that they would get a better price for their pelts." One attempt to stop this fraternization between the French and British on the Ohio Valley area was the establishment of Fort St. Vincent (thought to be located on the Ohio River in the southern Illinois area) in 1702, by Charles Jurchereau de Saint Denys. Its purpose was to be a tannery to process 12,000 buffalo skins and to help open a new route between Quebec and New Orleans. The older route through Chicago and the Illinois River was becoming hazardous because of the belligerence of the Fox Indians. However, Fort St. Vincent was abandoned in 1704 after an epidemic killed off most of the French and the Indians hired to man the post. The survivors of the epidemic become discouraged and left.

By 1712, the Indians were secretly trading with the British who were paying twice the French rate for pelts. Other Indians were traveling far down the Wabash and Scioto rivers to seek out the English traders from Pennsylvania, Virginia and the Carolinas.

The French King leased the mineral rights to Antoine Crozat for 15 years in 1712 because the Louisiana Colony was a money loser for the crown. Crozat gave up his lease after five years because he could not find the gold and silver minerals he had expected. The colony was taken over by John Law's Company of the West which later merged into the Company of the Indies. About this time, the French brought miners into the Mississippi watershed to explore for and remove minerals. They were looking for gold and silver but found lead, copper, iron and coal. Some of the dry caves were worked at a later date for the bat droppings from which they could obtain saltpeter for gunpowder.

The Illinois Country was annexed by Louisiana on September 27, 1717, with vaguely defined northern boundaries. The area that later became the Illinois Country of the Northwest Territory continued to send furs down the Mississippi during the time the explorers were conducting their search for mineral wealth.

The English traders were encouraged to invade the Ohio and Wabash valleys to collect furs on the site of the Indian hunting grounds by their east coast buyers. By 1715, the French again allowed their fur buyers to trade in the villages of the Wabash Valley because of the report that English traders were working that area. An unknown number of French men had intermarried with the Indians and lived in the Indian villages with their wives. Their subtle influence was felt until the War of 1812. During the 150 years of French dominance in North America, there were no more than 100,000 total French citizens. Most of these were in Canada. Less than 2,000 French were in the Northwest Territory at this time.

In 1719, the governor of Canada authorized two new posts on the Wabash: Fort Ouiatenon and Vincennes. One of the reasons for the French establishment of Fort Ouiatenon was to counter the recent British establishment of houses and stores on an effluent of the Wabash River. The French encouraged the Indians of southern Indiana to move closer to Fort Ouiatenon to remove them from the British trader's influence. In 1725, the governor of Montreal in his report to Paris mentioned "two houses and some stores" which "the English from Carolina" had built "on a little river which flows into the Ouabache, where they trade with the Miamis and the Ouyatanons." Quiatenon remained an occupied post until its destruction in 1763 by the Indians in Pontiac's War.

By 1730, after the settlement of Vincennes had been established and the Piankashaw Indians were settling near the post, Vincennes became a fur trading post sending out 30,000 skins a year. Sub posts were said to be located at French Store (north east of Brownstown), French Lick, Port Royal (Waverly), Tassinong (a Potawatomi village) and other places. Many of the early French trappers and traders were not registered with the officials in Quebec. These men were known as "Coureurs de bois" or woods rangers. Their numbers and whereabouts were unknown. Game and fur were plentiful in this area at that time, and fur was what these men were after. When the Americans moved into the Fort Vallonia area in 1807, they found an abandoned trading post. It consisted of the trading house and twelve cabins in three neat rows of four houses each.

In 1734, a large number of Miami Indians left the Wabash Valley to attack the Chickasaw Indians in Mississippi. They returned to that area again in 1736 with thirty soldiers, 100 voyagers and colonists, some Wea and Iroquois Indians as well as almost all of the Kaskaskia Indians. The Chickasaws had gotten word they were coming and were ready for them. They soundly defeated them and captured the French leaders, whom they tortured and burnt at the stake. The French governor of Louisiana realized the seriousness of the situation and sent 43 soldiers to replace those lost as well as 200 French, Indians and Negroes to the Illinois and Indiana posts.

In 1737, the Louisiana officials reported to the crown that the cost of keeping Vincennes open was more than it was worth, but it must be done to keep the British from taking over that area. These men kept their business very secret as to where they were really trading with the Indians. They knew that many others would like to cut into their trade areas if they could just figure where they had been so successful.

In 1741, De Noyan wrote at Detroit that "The English have been coming for a number of years to corrupt the Savages within the sphere of this post and I have resolved to have them pillaged." By 1744, the fight for the fur trade of the Ohio and Wabash valleys was bitter. Three years later, the French were having a revolt among the Miami. They seized eight French traders at the Miami post, looted the property and burned part of the buildings. The Indians of Indiana Territory were told to abandon the French or they would be killed. The French tried to label these statements as false rumors and put the blame for the uprising on the presence of the English and the lack of trade goods at the French posts. The new English trading post at Piqua, Ohio, was doing good trade with high pelt prices and low trade good prices.

By 1748, it is estimated that 300 English traders were working the greater Ohio Valley area. They were trading guns, powder, bar lead, duffels, knives, flints, shirts, gartering, vermillion, looking glasses, brass kettles, hatchets, rings, medals blades, ribbon, Dutch pipes, jointed babies, hats, shoes, tin pots, stockings, hoes, scissors, combs, needles, rum, half ticks, Jew's harps, etc., all of British manufacture

"Long Hunters" were men who would go into the wilds west of the Cumberland Gap for up to two years to hunt fur. One of the early "Long Hunters" in 1754 was James McBride. He left his name and date carved on a tree in Kentucky. In 1767, another to travel down to the Falls of the Ohio was John Finley. He is the man credited with interesting Daniel Boone in the wonders of Kentucky.

The Wyandotte chief, Nicholas, moved 120 of his warriors and their families to the White River system from Sandusky, Ohio, in 1748. The Huron (also known as the Wyandotte) invited the Delaware and Shawnee to settle north of the Ohio River before 1750.

The Miami Indians and their sub groups of Piankashaw, Wea and Potawatomi claimed the Wabash River valley and its tributaries as their territory. The French had by 1749 installed a permanent commandant at Detroit which had authority over the Miami, La Riviere Blanch (White River), Ouiatanon and the Wabash nations. The loyalty of the Weas to the French was being questioned by the French in 1749. By 1751, it was feared by Francois-Marie le Marchand de Ligneris in his report that the Piankashaw were about to change their allegiance to the English if the French did not make a major effort to control the Ohio River area.

In 1751, open war developed and the English and their Indian allies were driven out. Many of the Miami helped Beaujeu in the destruction of Braddock, and many young warriors joined in the raids of the Virginia and Pennsylvania frontiers. In 1755, the commandant of the Wea post reported that his Indians were ready to assist in the eastern raids. The next spring 250 Miami and Ouiatanon braves were at Fort Duquesne (Pittsburgh). They helped in raids that killed or captured three hundred persons. Some English prisoners were brought back to the villages.

The French realized they needed a fort at the Falls of the Ohio to keep the British out in 1757, but could not build one due to lack of manpower and resources. Fort Miami was shipping 250 to 300 packages of pelts in 1757. The Miami who traded at this post had about 160 warriors. The same year Ouiatanon was producing 300 to 400 packages of pelts from the 300 Wea, Kickapoo, Muscatine and Piankashaw warriors. Vincennes was producing 80 packages of pelts from the Piankashaw there. Some of the fur trade from Vincennes was going to both the English and the Spanish in Missouri.

At this time the Indians of the west were not subdued, but by the surrender of Montreal in 1760 the control of the west changed from French to English. The Indians in this area were not happy about the change. Their feelings led to Pontiac's War in 1763 against Detroit and the upper Ohio Territory. What happened to the British traders in the Indiana area at this time has not been recorded. The English fur traders were, for the most part, the worst class of men.

There were only a handful of British soldiers in Indiana and they were 1,000 miles from reinforcements and supplies. The British soldiers were wholly unfitted by their training for the western service. In spite of the English short comings in the territory, the French influence waned from the Wabash and Ohio River valleys in 1764. While the immediate cause of French defeat in the Northwest was English military success in Canada, the deeper cause was the type of government they used in this area, the monopoly of trade which stifled free enterprise, the over expansion of the area they tried to control, and the corruption of their officials.

The French did not leave an abiding influence in Indiana except in stream and place names. But they had planted the seeds of destruction in the Indian tribes. They had introduced the dependency on trade goods, European sickness and diseases, and a strong desire for liquor.

The French continued to think that they had rights to the Northwest Territory as late as 1798. President Adams sent three commissioners to France, but word arrived that the French Foreign Minister Talleyrand and the Directory had refused to negotiate with them unless the U.S. opened the port of New Orleans, returned the Northwest Territory, and paid a large sum of money before talks could begin. Adams reported the insult to Congress, and the Senate printed the correspondence, in which the Frenchmen were referred to only as "X, Y, and Z."

The British tried to do away with the gifts the agents gave to the tribes to gain their favor. This had been the French custom in dealing with the Indians and had been part of the reason for poor profits from the territory. Without the gifts, the British had a hard time in controlling the country. The first attempt by the British to send an expedition up the Mississippi River and into the Illinois Country in the spring of 1764 was unsuccessful because unfriendly Indians turned them back. Captain Thomas Morris, with a group of friendly Indians and two French guides, tried to enter the country from Detroit. They were intercepted by Chief Pontiac and some Indians. Only through the efforts of the French guides was Morris's life spared. He went on to Fort Miami where he was again threatened with death by the Indians. The local chief intervened but warned him not to try to go to Fort Ouianton. He turned back to join Colonel Bradstreet in Detroit.

Next the route down the Ohio River was tried by George Croghan. He was taken prisoner by the Mascouten and Kickapoo Indians near the mouth of the Wabash River. After being taken to Vincennes and later to Ouiatanon, Croghan was released and talked peace and trade with the Indians at several Indian councils. Pontiac took part in these meetings but steadfastly maintained that the English could not take over the land title from the French since the French were only tenants on Indian grounds. While Croghan was in Vincennes, he recognized that place as a potential important trading post. He said it was "a place of great consequence for Trade being a fine hunting country all along the Ouabache and too far for the Indians which reside there to go either to the Illinois or elsewhere to fetch their necessaries." At this time the Miami Indians were complaining that they must go to Detroit for everything, even for shirts and leggings; and since they had no blacksmiths to repair their guns and tomahawks, how could they support their families? They also complained of traders bringing brandy to their villages and begged that this not be permitted.

In 1764, tribal estimates of warriors in Indiana were Potawatomi, Eel River and Kickapoo, 300; Mascouten, 90; Miami, 250; Piankashaw, 250; Wea, 300; Choctaw, whose numbers were unknown; and Delaware, who were not yet in Indiana Territory and left in 1818. The Delaware moved into the west fork of White River and established 14 village sites along a fifty-mile run of White River from near Noblesville to near Muncie. The major villages were at Muncie and Anderson.

The Company of Baynton, Wharton and Morgan in Pittsburgh sent supplies to start a trading post in 1768 to Vincennes. Some of the goods are thought to have been plundered on the way to the post and the store was plundered the next year by the Indians. The agent, Alexander Williamsons, was not heard of again until 1771. He was on the Mississippi at Cahokia. Details of how he got there are unknown. The British abandoned plans for trade garrisons on the Wabash in 1768 and turned the trade problem over to the individual colonies. One trader, Patrick Morgan of Kaskaskia, is reported to have shipped down the Mississippi 14,000 deerskins and assorted other animal skins in 1773.

In September of 1770, General Gage reported to Johnson that the "Ouabache Indians instead of becoming more peaceable have grown worse; and the navigation of the Ohio will be more precarious daily, unless some measures are taken to bring them to reason." The following year, Gage reported that neither the Potawatomi nor the tribes on the Wabash would suffer an English trader to come amongst them. For this hostility he blamed the French who were "thick" on that stream. In response to his complaint, the British secretary informed Gage that it was the King's pleasure that the French be removed. After receiving the order, Gage was slow to implement it because he did not want to offend the Indians. The French petitioned for relief since they had lived on the land for a long time and had clear title to it from the French government. Proof of this title was still being discussed when the British were removed from Vincennes during the Revolutionary War.

Lieutenant Governor Edward Abbott left Detroit on April 15, 1777, to set up a post at Vincennes, but had no garrison to man it. The Indians expected Abbott to make gifts along the way down the Wabash to his post. The Indians said the French always gave them more, but let him pass anyway. No British official had taken control of Vincennes in the fourteen years it had been in their possession. This was a place of lawlessness by all concerned. Abbott organized three militia companies of a total of 150 men but had no fort. The Indians visited the town regularly in groups of up to 300 braves. He thought the Indians' purpose was to set the French inhabitants against the British government. Abbott stockaded his cabin and this may be the site of the later Fort Sackville that Clark took from Hamilton. Governor Carleton severely criticized Abbott for his gifts to the Indians, which were a drain on the governor's budget. The rebuke caused Abbott to stop trying to buy the Indians' assistance and friendship. On September 26, he wrote that he had stopped all expenses, except the pay of the interpreters. "I lately received advice from Indians of different Nations, [that] the Rebels intend to attack on this place. Should they succeed it will render them masters of the Wabache and of course procure them the interests of the Indians on this river." Finally, on February 3, 1778, Abbott left Vincennes, and after a 33-day journey to Detroit, resigned his lieutenant governorship. One of his written complaints to Lord Germain concerned the use of the Indians against the helpless settlers.

Hamilton's own figures of the number of scalping parties clearly reveal the inhumanity of Indian warfare. He reported that seven parties of Indians with white leaders had been dispatched by July 18, 1777, totaling 178 warriors and 22 white officers, an average of 25 Indians and three officers to each party. During the next nine days, 111 more warriors were sent to the frontier. By September 5, 1777, Hamilton reported he had dispatched seven hundred warriors and that an additional 450 had been dispatched by other officers.

There were 8,000 Indians in the Northwest Territory under the loose control of the British. George Washington wanted to strike at Detroit and neutralize the British control of them, but he could not get there to attack the town. The British wanted just as much to encourage the Indians to take up the hatchet and kill the American frontiersman and his family during the revolution.

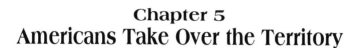

Chapter 5
Americans Take Over the Territory

By 1780, when the new American government had taken over the Indiana Territory, the traders had to register with them. Some who had been active long before that time were registered to the following areas: Mr. Todd, Blue River, Washington County; Conner brothers, White River; Joseph Dumay, White River; and Jonnet Pillet on White River.

With the Revolutionary War over, there was a change of administration of the Indians in the west. The Congress of the Confederation officially proclaimed an end to hostilities on April 11, 1783. They sent a messenger to Detroit to communicate through the British to the Indians that they should look to the United States as their "father." The British stalled in allowing the Indians to be gathered and told of the peace negotiations between the United States and Britain. The Indians heard the rumors and were deeply troubled. At Detroit, a delegation of Wea and Kickapoo requested a meeting with the British commander, De Peyster, on June 28 where they expressed their uneasiness over the rumors. "We are informed that instead of prosecuting the war, we are to give up our lands to the Enemy, in endeavoring to assist you it seems we have wrought our own ruin," the Wea spokesman declared. Though their services were no longer needed, they expressed the hope that the British would continue to supply their wants. De Peyster wrote that "whole villages" of other nations were on the way to Detroit, "impatient to know what is to become of them and their lands" and to request a supply of goods.

The English superintendent of Indian affairs met with representatives of the Indians and assured them that the King still considered them his faithful children. They were not to believe that the treaty would deprive them of their "right of soil" established in 1768 by the Treaty of Fort Stanwix, nor did he believe that the United States would try to deprive them of any part of their country. He advised them to bear their losses with fortitude, forgive and forget what was past. He sealed his statement by giving presents to the Indians.

On October 15, 1783, the Continental Congress adopted a report which said that the Indians were a defeated nation and had no right to the soil on which they lived. The new government in the colonies tried to subdue the Indians for the next twenty years with some success at some times and little success at other times. One of their main tactics was to send out a large group of men on horseback and seek out Indian villages, destroy the food crops and, hopefully, engage the warriors and kill enough of them to discourage further Indian raids on the whites.

On March 4, 1784, five commissioners were appointed to negotiate with the Indians. The five who accepted were Richard Butler, George Rogers Clark, Benjamin Lincoln, Arthur Lee and Oliver Wolcott; only three served at any one time. They drove such a hard bargain in their negotiations with the Indians that the Indians wanted to reject the land treaties because the whole tribe had not ratified the decision of a few chiefs who they felt had been bullied into giving up more than the tribes thought proper. The entire Indian confederacy wanted to renew the negotiations but only on the basis of the Ohio River being the boundary between themselves and the whites.

The Indians held a grand war council at Ouiatenon in August 1785. Their purpose was to plan driving out all Americans north of the Ohio and make general war against Kentucky.

The Miami were the sponsor of the council. At this time the settlers were starting to settle on the south bank of the Ohio. The Indians had retreated to the north bank of White River. This left about a forty-mile void between the whites and the red skins. This territory left some "breathing room" between the two groups, but they were close enough to each other that they would organize raids and counter raids into the other's territory.

The French citizens of Vincennes were terrorized in the spring of 1786 when the Wabash Indians and the Americans were fighting along the Wabash River. The French were trying to act as arbitrators between the Indians and Americans but were having little success. The Indians, on the warpath, made little difference between the Americans and the English because of the English abandoning them after urging them to take up the ax during the American Revolution. Filson wrote George Rogers Clark at the request of the French and American citizens of Vincennes on March 16, 1786. They needed help before they were all killed by the Indians. The Indians had scalped one settler near Vincennes and destroyed the crops and promised to return in the fall to finish their work. The people of Kentucky were reluctant to leave their homes to fight the Indians unless they were actually threatened by the tribes. Clark knew this and asked Congress for part of General Harmar's federal troops to help with this emergency. Congress refused, but Patrick Henry, governor of Virginia, sent instructions for 2,000 men and materials to be drafted for the cause. Clark was not happy with this arrangement because he had used drafted men before and thought it was a disaster in the making. He reluctantly took command of the 1,200 who did show up. He wanted to go directly to the Indian towns on the Wabash, but was overruled and had to wait at Vincennes for his supplies to arrive by water. They were late and the beef ration had spoiled. The drafted men became mutinous on the second day of march to the Indian towns and the majority set out for their homes when they got within one day of the villages. Clark returned to Vincennes and tried to figure out how to put the best face on his failure. He was afraid if the Indians knew what really happened, they would be encouraged to do vast damage to the settlers in Indiana since they felt there was nothing to fear from the Kentucky Militia. He sent word to the Wabash tribes to come to Clarksville for a powwow in November. If they did not come, he would accept their absence as a desire for war. One of the French sent word to the Indians that Clark had started to their villages with an army, but he had talked Clark into giving the Indians one last chance to sit and talk peace before Clark wiped them out. The chiefs were slow to reply, but when they did they stated they did not want to go to Clarksville but would meet with Clark at Vincennes in April. Since this was a bluff on Clark's part, he accepted; it would also help insure a relatively quiet winter for the settlers. Clark reported the mutinous activity and the spring meeting to the Virginia governor. He left it to others as to what would happen at the spring meeting.

At this time it appeared that from a disaster he had negotiated a major treaty meeting to settle the fate of Indiana. Then James Wilkinson stepped in and sent trumped up charges that included drunkenness and illegal confiscation of the supplies of a Spanish trader that were converted to Clark's military needs to the Virginian governor Benjamin V. Harrison. The governor's support was withdrawn from Clark.

In 1786, Governor Benjamin Harrison of Virginia was dealing with several problems. The primary problem he confronted was money—as in other colonies, the coffers of the Virginia treasury were drained by the war and the government was plagued by creditors, both domestic and foreign. It was clear that there was no capacity for military action outside of the immediate area, so Harrison steadfastly opposed offensive action sought against Indians in the Kentucky and Illinois country. Wilkinson's allegations were readily accepted as a reason to dismiss Clark.

Congress also heard of the charges and would not allow the federal troops to help at Vincennes. The meeting fell through and Clark's reputation was badly tarnished.

Colonel Harmar did go to Vincennes in the summer of 1787 to investigate the situation and he decided to start Fort Knox under the command of Hamtramck with two companies of federal troops. Fort Knox was built a few hundred yards north of the older Fort Patrick Henry (old Fort Sackville). Later Fort Knox was moved two miles up river to the top of a bluff overlooking the river. While Hamtramck was in command at Vincennes for five years, some law and order was finally enforced there, but he could not stop the Indians from making raids into Kentucky nor stop Kentuckians from making counter-raids.

The federal government was coming to the position in treaties with the Indians that the tribes had a "right to the soil" and met with some two hundred Iroquois, Wyandotte, Delaware, Ottawa, Chippewa and Potawatomi in December of 1788 to renegotiate some land treaties. The Indians still wanted the Ohio River as their southern boundary. Governor St. Clair stood firm against this wish, but did give the western Indians an additional $6,000 in goods and reconfirmed the boundaries settled earlier at Fort McIntosh. The treaties were signed on January 9, 1789. The treaties were similar to the 1785 treaties. Again the tribal members thought their representatives had been bullied into giving too much for what they received in return. Most of the Wabash and Illinois Indians had not been represented at the Fort Harmar meeting and did not feel obliged to follow the treaty. Their raids continued with little or no interruption.

On August 26, 1789, Colonel John Hardin and 200 troops left Fort Steuben at Jeffersonville for raids on Indian towns on the Wabash. They returned on September. 28 without a casualty. At some time during this period of time of 1789, Hardin and his men surrounded a fort at the junction of the Mascatatuck and White rivers. The supposed British occupants abandoned the fort and are thought to have retreated to the north.

President Washington made one more attempt to sound out the peace or war intentions of the Wabash Indians. In 1789, he instructed the Northwest Territory Governor Arthur St. Clair to determine the intent of the Indians. St. Clair sent Antoine Gamelin to the villages with the president's message in April 1790. Most villages were noncommittal and said the decision rested with the Miami. At a meeting with the Miami, Delaware and Shawnee at the Miami village of Kekionga, Gamelin was told that the decision could not be made until the British at Detroit had been consulted. Gamelin went no further and returned to Vincennes. He reported to Governor St. Clair that it was not possible to obtain a peace with the Indians. Some of the younger warriors had already taken to the warpath.

In September 1790, a plan was devised for a two-prong attack on the Indians of northern Indiana. Hamtramck was to lead troops up the Wabash from Vincennes while General Harmar was to attack the Fort Wayne area from Cincinnati. General Harmar led an army of 320 regular army and approximately 1,200 Kentucky militia. They reached the Miami villages on October 17. No armed resistance was encountered as the Indians had fled into the forest. The army did burn their village and plunder their stores. Two Indian villages 18 miles up the St. Joseph River were hit by Colonel John Hardin. Miami Chief Little Turtle trapped Hardin troops there and many were captured and tortured. It was late in the season, supplies were short, the pack horses were dying for lack of food. After the defeat of Hardin's men, General Harmar thought it best to return to Fort Washington (Cincinnati). This defeat and retreat encouraged the Indians into greater activity against the whites. A diversionary force of militia was organized and set out from Vincennes. At the same time, Harmar was setting out from Fort Washington. Hamtramck set out with 330 men to the Vermilion village. He found no Indians. His men were on short supplies and the soldiers and French civilians were restless to return to their homes. The expedition was called off. No military action had been initiated. However, Hamtramck was later informed that 600 Wabash Indian braves had been waiting further up the river to ambush his men. The 600 braves had been diverted from the Fort Wayne area, and that had relieved some of the pressure on General Harmar's army at that point. The Indians boasted to General Putnam that "there should not remain a Smoak on the Ohio by the time the leaves put out," i.e., by the spring of 1791, no fires would burn in the settlers cabins. Some of the settlers moved into the few stockade forts. Others left the area for the east and safety.

On May 23, 1791, Brigadier General Charles Scott started out on a raid by crossing the Ohio River east of Madison with 800 mounted and armed men. This march was known as the "Blackberry Campaign." A short distance from the Ouiatanon village of the Wea they were discovered by a lone Indian who rode to his tribe to sound the alarm. Colonel John Hardin's group attacked a Kickapoo village on his side of the river and killed six Indians and took fifty two women and children as prisoners. The river was too flooded for Scott to cross at that point to gain the Ouiatanon village. They had to ford the stream at another point. When they got to the village, it was deserted. The next day, Colonel James Wilkinson took 360 men across the river and attacked the Indian town of Tippecanoe 18 miles to the north. He destroyed the village and returned to the main body in twelve hours. Several French were living at the Tippecanoe village in quite civilized homes. They had books and letters in their homes and had neat gardens and a tavern in the village. Wilkinson reported that he had burnt about seventy houses, many well finished. On June 14, Scott returned to Fort Steuben with 41 prisoners from action on the west fork of White River, the Eel, and the Miami rivers, which he turned over to Captain Asheton. He had released sixteen prisoners who were too sick to travel.

Colonel John Armstrong was commander of Fort Steuben (Jeffersonville) for several years (est. 1787-1790) and his tombstone states that while there he made frequent excursions against the Indians; however, the dates and locations of those excursions were not listed. John Bakless mentioned in his book *America As Seen By Its First Explorers* that John Armstrong was sent on a secret mission by the army in 1790 to explore the Missouri to its source and all its southern branches. The army did not even inform the president, Thomas Jefferson, of this mission. Armstrong and his party were to be "habited like Indians in all respects" and were to conceal their illicit presence in the Spanish Territory. Armstrong got no further than St. Louis and St. Genevieve.

In August, James Wilkinson marched north from Cincinnati and attacked the Miami village of Little Turtle. He returned through Tippecanoe and Ouiatanon where he burned the fields of garden crops to shorten the Indians' winter food supplies. He then returned to Fort Steuben after a raid as successful as Scott's. Some of the Wabash Indians sought peace as a result of these raids. In April 1792, Wilkinson sent two emissaries to the Maumee to try to gain peace with them. However, with the defeat of St. Clair's 1,400-man mob by Little Turtle's 1,000 warriors in a dawn attack on November 4, the Indians were in no mood to talk peace. They had killed 600 of St. Clair's men and wounded another 200. They captured Wilkinson's messengers. Captain Alexander Trueman had a peace message from the Secretary of War for the western Indians and Colonel John Hardin had a similar message for the Wyandotte. Both men were killed by the Indians before they could deliver their messages.

General Rufus Putnam had instructions to hold a council at Maumee during the summer of 1792. He changed the location to Vincennes after hearing of the killing of the other peace emissaries. He met with 680 from the Eel River Miami, Wea, Potawatomi, Kickapoo, Piankashaw, Muscatine and Kaskaskia. Putnam and the Indians agreed on a Peace Treaty, but the U.S. Senate refused to ratify it on January 4, 1794.

The government sent men to Detroit in June 1793 to reconfirm the Treaty of 1783 and, if necessary, give the Indians more money to seal the bargain. They did acknowledge that the United States did not obtain the lands from the English, only the exclusive rights to buy the land from the Indians. The Indians were in council at Maumee. When they did meet with Putnam, they had upped the price for peace. They wanted their boundary to be the Ohio River. They stated that no agreement would be binding unless agreed to by all the tribes in a general council. In regard to the money, they replied, "Money, to us, is of no value, and to most is unknown.... We want Peace...restore to us our country and we shall be enemies no longer.... We consider ourselves free to make any bargain or cession of lands, whenever and to whomever we please." They suggested that the money be given to those who had settled on the disputed land in order to get them to move away.

When the results of the council was made known at Philadelphia, Wayne was authorized to renew hostilities. War Secretary Knox wrote, "Every effort has been made to obtain peace by milder terms than the sword—the efforts have failed under circumstances which leave nothing for us to expect but war." War was expected by both sides. Wayne trained his new army and the British armed the Indians and built a fort on supposed American soil. After the Battle of Fallen Timbers, Wayne confronted the nearby fort commander. Each challenged the right of the other to be at this place, but neither fired on the other. It is thought they both knew of Jay's peace negotiations going on at that time in London and did not want to start a general war when peace might occur with the diplomats.

Wayne had three goals in his campaign. The first was to defeat the Indians, which he did at the Battle of Fallen Timbers on August 20, 1794. The second was to build a military fort, which was completed at Fort Wayne on October 22. The third was to obtain a treaty with the Indians. This was obtained in the Treaty of Greenville on August 3, 1795. This treaty was with the Wyandotte, Delaware, Shawnee, Miami, Ottawa, Chippewa, Potawatomi, Wea, Kickapoo, Eel River Miami, Piankashaw and Kaskaskia. This treaty opened up part of southeastern Indiana for settlement as well as the portage areas, Ouiatenon, Clark's Grant and the Vincennes Tract. For this the Indians got

$20,000 in trade goods and an annual dividend of $9,000. This treaty also obtained the release of many settlers captured by the Indians. Some of those released had been captured in Indiana territory. Some of these men were John Brown, captured in 1791 near Falls of the Ohio; James Burge, captured in 1791 at Clarksville; David Spangler, age 22, captured December 9, 1794, at the Falls, surrendered back on September 14, 1795, by Potawatomies; Peter Smith, captured 1793 near Falls of the Ohio, released 1795 by Potawatomies; Samuel Thorn Jr., 20, captured at the Falls of the Ohio in March 1790, surrendered June 5, 1795, by the Potawatomies.

Indian abductions were still occurring on the trails. The Larkin family was attacked near Jasper, Indiana, at a place known as the Mudholes in southern Indiana. The head of the family was killed. His wife and five children were captured. Mrs. Larkin was the daughter of Colonel Greenup, a prominent Kentucky official. Greenup mounted a massive search for his daughter and her children and they were finally rescued. The last murder in Clark County by Indians was by the Wyandotte and Pawpaw Indians. The victim was named Springer and was killed in New Albany in the first decade of the 1800's. About the same time, the Choctaw Indians in Martin County are rumored to have had a great battle and hastily left the area.

Harrison wrote to the Secretary of War in July 1801, about the Indians of the Wabash. He said, "I do not believe that there are no more than six hundred warriors upon the (Wabash) river and yet the quantity of whiskey brought here annually for their use is said to amount to at least six thousand gallons." He further wrote, "Their Chiefs and their nearest relations fall under the strokes of their tomahawks and knives. This has been so much the case with the three tribes nearest us—the Piankashaws, Weas, and the Eel River Miami—that there is scarcely a Chief to be found amongst them." These tribes had also rescinded the land rights of the Delaware Indians to the upper White River area. The Delaware's pride was deeply hurt by this and they were thinking of moving to west of the Mississippi with another Delaware clan encampment. This year, smallpox broke out among the Kickapoo and reduced their number.

In 1801, the Moravian missionaries who had come among the Delaware Indians of the White River were attempting to teach them how to farm by European methods. They asked Harrison to control the traders and not allow them to sell liquor within ten miles of any of their settlements. Many of the Delaware Indians were intrigued by the new religion and talked about it much. However, many came to the conclusion that the Brethren had been sent by the whites just to make the Indians tame, so that they might be killed, as had been done at the Gnadenhutten Mission. The Indians were afraid of becoming tame, because it took away from them the only defense they knew against hostile intruders, whether they were whites or other Indians.

Tecumseh's brother, the "Prophet," appeared at the Moravian mission and accused the Delaware converts of being bewitched by white man's magic. He burned some converts at the stake. After the burning of the brethren, the Moravians closed the mission and left on September 16, 1806.

Moravian missionary Abraham Lukenbach wrote of his experience with the Indians: "The Chiefs addressed their people, both men and women, and, although they themselves did not abstain, strictly prohibited the use of strong drink, fornication, adultery, stealing, lying, cheating, murder, and urged hospitality, love, unity as things well pleasing to God, which is proof that even the heathen is not without knowledge of good and evil and therefore has a conscience.... It was customary among them...to visit and greet one another with a mutual handshake. In connection with this, they assumed a solemn mien and used courtly language according to the age or circumstances of the family addressed. All this made a good show to one who does not know them or their circumstances. But after one has made a closer acquaintance with them, one learns, unfortunately, how they distrust one another, even their nearest relatives, because of poisoning, witchcraft, and black art, so that really not one confides in another. The fellowship of love is therefore unknown among them, and on such occasions they merely make a pretense, because they are really afraid of one another."

Lukenbach went on to say that the Indians believed that "God had indeed given the bible to the white people...but to the Indians...He had given the hunting grounds, sacrificial feasts, and had shown them another mode of life," and they were of the opinion that "the Indians did not come from the same source as the white people, but had been created separately, for which reason they were not allowed to adopt the customs of the white people." He went on to say that some Indians "declare that because of the acceptance of the white man's religion on the part of some, their gods had become angry and sought their destruction; that their deities wanted to take away from them their land and all customs and liberties, including the use of whisky, which was the discovery of the whites, as well as their silver and gold, and the practice of usury among them, all of which they regarded as an evil in the world, and as originally unknown among the race, and something that had been brought upon them by the white people."

Experiments were made by the American people to "civilize" some of the Indians by giving them schooling in American schools. Usually the results were not what was expected. One Miami chief, George White Eyes, who had been educated at Princeton, was asked why he returned to the savage ways of his tribe. He stated, "It is natural we should follow the footsteps of our forefathers, and when you white people undertake to direct us from this path, you learn us to eat, drink, dress, read and write like yourselves, and then you turn us loose to beg, starve or seek our native forests, without alternative and outlawed by your society, we curse you for the feelings you have taught us, and resort to excesses that we may forget them."

Some of the Indian leaders of the early days of contact with the Europeans were of mixed race births. One such leader was a renowned chief and orator, Red Jacket. His mother was a white taken prisoner by the Indians. However, even with mixed heritage he was very critical of the white man's religion. Red Jacket made a speech in New York about the feelings of the Indians for the white man's religion. He stated that the "black coats" (missionaries) had come among his people, smiling and friendly, but had split the tribe into Christians and anti-Christians. Before the black coats had come, the tribe lived in peace and harmony with each other. Since the teachings had been presented, there had been bad feeling within the tribe and several of the Christian Indians had taken up the white trader's habits of lying and cheating the rest of the tribe. Red Jacket said that when the Quakers came, they treated the Indians with kindness and gave them plows and taught them how to use farming implements. However, the Quakers did not demand that the Indians change their religion in exchange for the gifts, and they did not demand land concessions. With the Quakers, they could still honor their Great Spirit in the old ways.

Red Jacket said that white missionaries taught them to love the great father and his son. Red Jacket said the Indians did honor the Great Spirit. He pointed out that Jesus had not been killed by the Indians, who were heathens, but by those of his own group who believed in the Great Spirit that the missionaries wanted them to honor. Further note was made that the Indians did not want to convert the whites who came into their lands to their religion, but agreed that the whites should follow their own teachings. Since there were some new settlers in the area the missionaries were preaching to, his people would watch for a time and see how these people turned out in their dealings with the Indians of the area. Red Jacket thought that time would tell if the new people would lie, cheat and steal from the Indians as had the traders, or if they would treat the Indians according to the principles of the missionaries.

The Indian nations were frightened and perplexed about their future in this new society that the settlers were bringing to the Indians' land. They knew the Indians were in a "war of attrition." With each calamity there were fewer of them. Yet every month more whites came into their cherished forests to settle. The Indians were a fierce, proud and desperate people, yet they were at times a meek and timid people, confused by the continual culture clash with the whites that gave them no peace.

The Indian tribes were aware of the calamity that they were facing with continued war with a new civilization on their land. They had fought for centuries with other tribes. Some of the former great tribes had been weakened by the fights and forced to wander in the outback; they were considered as second class citizens by the dominate eastern tribes. They thought their future would repeat the past experiences as they faced this new foe (the whites) who came with many fighters, stayed on the land all the time and gave the Indians no place to retreat to.

The first few years of the 19th century saw several land treaties with the Indians. Harrison traveled to Fort Wayne and obtained a treaty for the land near Vincennes called the Vincennes Tract on June 7, 1803. It was signed by Chiefs Richardville and Little Turtle for the Miami. Topenbee and Winamac signed for the Potawatomi, Eel River, Wea, Piankashaw and Kaskaskia. Others signing were two Kickapoo, two Shawnee and four Delaware chiefs. Shortly after this treaty, the Indians met in council and stated that the Delaware had title to the lands between the White River and the Ohio River. The Delaware nation was made up of three tribes: the Turtle, the Turkey and the Wolf. Each tribe had its own chief and tribal officers.

The title to the land between the Ohio River, the Wabash River, and the Vincennes Road to the Falls of the Ohio was settled in the Treaty at Vincennes on August 27, 1804, with the Delaware. The government also recognized the sole rights of the Delaware to another parcel of land going to the Ohio boundary that the Miami contested. Harrison called a council at Vincennes with the Miami, Eel River, Wea, Delaware and Potawatomi. Harrison obtained the rights of all these in the Treaty at Grouseland, August 21, 1805. Fort Alexander at Vallonia was established in 1807. Its primary purpose was to be a ranger post for excursions against the Indians north and west of this post. Over seventy settler families had settled at the "forks" of the White and Muscatatuck rivers prior to the War of 1812; however, only twenty-three families remained until the war was over. The common name of Fort Alexander was Fort Vallonia since it was located in the village of Vallonia. The main trail to white civilization was to the Ohio River through Springville and Charlestown. A few Piankashaw were still living south of the Muscatatuck River, but most had been forced down the White River by earlier settler activity. The feared terrors of the area were the Kickapoo raiders from Illinois.

The Shawnee Indian Lauleswasika experienced a life-changing trance in 1805 and claimed to have spoken to the master of life while in the trance. In November of 1805, he proclaimed himself as the prophet of his people at a tribal council at Wapakoneta, Ohio. He began preaching to the Indians the need to put off the white man's ways and return to old beliefs. He and his brother Tecumseh took their followers to Greenville, Ohio, where they attracted a large group of Indians interested in following the "Prophet." The Prophet moved his headquarters to *keth-tip-pe-can-nunk*, also known as Prophet's Town and Tippecanoe, in 1808.

The Treaty at Fort Wayne on August 30, 1809, fanned the flames of Indian resentment toward continued white intrusion into their lands. The Potawatomi and Delaware were willing to cede more land. The Miami were not so ready. The Wea and Kickapoo would also have to agree to the ceding of land north of Vincennes. The Prophet and Tecumseh stated to the Indians that no one tribe could agree to cede any land. It took a general council of all the Indians to agree to such a move. They were afraid that the Indians were being negotiated out of their land and would have nowhere to go if they continued to take trade goods and trinkets for the land. Tecumseh was becoming of the opinion that it was impossible to remain friends with the United States unless the government was willing to abandon the idea of extending settlements and acknowledge the principle that all western lands were the common property of all the tribes. The 1809 treaty opened up three million acres in south central Indiana for settlement. This area included most of Jackson, Lawrence, Martin, Monroe, Green, Clay, Owen, Sullivan and Vigo counties. The line ran from Raccoon Creek on the Wabash to a point west of Seymour on what is now U.S. Highway 50. The northern boundary of this treaty was called the Ten O'Clock Line because the sun's shadow would lie directly on this straight line at ten o'clock in the morning on every September 30 (the day of the treaty signing). This was the treaty that made Tecumseh famous because he let it be known that he did not think this treaty was valid since all the tribes did not agree to it. He threatened to kill and scalp all the chiefs who had signed the treaty and all the settlers who would settle on the land involved.

Harrison invited Tecumseh to a council at Vincennes in August 1810, to work out his objections to the treaty. Tecumseh came with representatives of the Delaware, Eel River, Kickapoo and Wea tribes and strongly voiced his objections. Both men agreed that they could not agree. Both began to prepare their side for war.

In July 1811, some Potawatomi Indians killed some settlers in Illinois. Harrison took the initiative and called for a council at Vincennes with Tecumseh in August. Harrison insisted that the Indians who had murdered the settlers were under the control and influence of the Prophet. After the council, Tecumseh headed south to gather the southern Indians for his army.

In the summer of 1811, General William Henry Harrison organized a search and destroy mission at the Falls of the Ohio. He charged young George Croghan of the Kentucky Rangers and 250 men with carrying out his policy. In August, they advanced into the future location of Lawrence County near what would become Fort Ritner. Croghan's men built a stockade near Fort Ritner on the ruins of a cabin whose builder and family had been killed by the Indians. While they were building the stockade, word was received that Tecumseh was holding a powwow in an Indian village near the junction of Clear Creek and Salt Creek (near the current location of the Lawrence–Monroe county line and west along the old Monon Railroad from where Indiana Highway 37 crosses Clear Creek).

A scouting party under Captain James Montgomery was sent to scout out the meeting area. They found a village of 98 lodges with several corn patches planted in the Clear Creek bottoms. While this was Delaware territory, the village was primarily made up of Mohican Indians who had been permitted to live in that area by the Delaware and Miami chief, Little Turtle. Other reports stated that Little Turtle's mother was of the Mohican tribe. The Mohicans were also known for their diplomatic abilities in negotiations between the Indian nations. The members of this tribe may have later moved to Canada.

As the troops started to scout the village, they were discovered and attacked by the Indians close to a place known as Hickory Mound. Captain Montgomery was killed by an arrow to the heart. David McHolland assumed command of the scouting party and dispatched their Indian guide, Ros-e-neah, back to Croghan's main camp for help. The scouting party took up a defensive position on a nearby cliff overlooking Clear Creek and, although almost all of the men were wounded, they held out for three days until Croghan's army arrived to reinforce their position. The ensuing battle resulted in 22 of Croghan's men killed with a defeat of the Mohican braves and their chief, Uncas.

Harrison gathered his army and arrived at Prophet's Town in November. Tecumseh had warned his brother not to attack the whites until he got back and the "Great Sign" had been observed. The Prophet could not wait and the result was the Battle of Tippecanoe. It is thought there was a total of 700 to 1,200 warriors from the Wea, Miami, Kaskaskia, Potawatomi, Wyandotte, Kickapoo, Winnebago, Ottawa, Chippewa, Sac and Shawnee tribes at the battle. Tecumseh was bringing another 2,000 braves, but they were not yet there when the Prophet started the battle. They were from the Choctaw, Creek and Chickasaw tribes. While many historians think the battle was inconclusive in a military sense, its premature timing did disrupt the plans of Tecumseh.

The "Great Sign" occurred on December 16, 1811. It was the New Madrid earthquake that made the Mississippi River run backwards, changed the course of the river, and destroyed the town of New Madrid, Missouri.

The Indians in Indiana were a paradoxical problem for the settlers. When the settlers first lived in Kentucky, they knew they were in trouble when they saw an Indian in the woods since most of the Indians lived north of the Ohio River. The white settler knew in his bones that he was in danger of losing his horse or a loved one when he saw an Indian shadow in the forest. However, in Indiana the ground rules were a little different. In many instances the settlers had moved into areas close to the Indian villages. It is not known if this was done because the Indians were at strategic locations of trails and resources or if the settlers (who were usually also militia members) were settling at forward observation posts to spy on the Indians and help control the few in the area before they could organize and raid settlers further to the south.

Many of the early settlers' children played with their red-skinned neighbors. They traded for the skins the Indians were so skillful at tanning. The Indians moved to the southern part of the state in large groups for the benefit of the milder winters than the cold and raw days on the northern Indiana plains. The illusion of peace and tranquility abounded from late fall through the winter. Surely, these people who appeared to be good-natured, mild-mannered and kind to children could not be the same who murdered the people in Kentucky only a few years earlier. However, some parts of the tribes could and did become violent when the time came to return north for the summer. It was very difficult to tell a good neighbor from a wild Indian, and several settlers paid the price of not maintaining their guard against a quick and violent band of Indians in southern Indiana.

In the spring of 1812, two hundred Delaware Indians were camped near Salem at Royce's Lick. Their chief was "Old Ox." One hundred more Indians were camped at Sparks Ferry near the Lawrence County line on White River. Other Indian villages in southern Indiana were those of King Billy, a Shawnee, and Killbuck, thought to be a Delaware Indian. King Billy had camps near Bedford and at the rise of Lost River in Orange County. The Killbuck village was in the Knobs north of Borden in Clark County.

During the times of peace between the Indians and the settlers, there were many social and hunting encounters between the warriors of both sides. They were known to greatly enjoy hunting together and on occasion have mutual admiration for each other. On one such occasion, after a successful hunt, the hunters were celebrating their good fortune with a healthy round of drinks. As they drank, both sides loosened up their tongues and started to recall the "good old days" of the conflicts. An Indian by the name of Silver Heels, who was one of the hunters at this gathering, started to recall his efforts in the conflict and told of killing and scalping 16 settlers. He made a particular point of telling of one man he had killed that had a double crown in his scalp and how he had tricked the British scalp buyer by cutting the scalp in such a way that he sold the single scalp as two scalps. He went on to describe in detail where and how he had killed the man. Two of the white hunters listened to his camp fire story with great interest. They thought the man he had killed was a relative of theirs. They went home and carefully verified the specific details Silver Heels had told and found them true in every detail. Silver Heels was found dead a few days later, shot through the head at his campsite.

On May 12, 1812, Indians from the Vincennes area led by the Indian "Pop in Dick" killed a Martin County gunsmith in his cabin bed at night. His name was John McGowan. The Boggs family had been killed and left in their burnt cabin a year earlier in the same neighborhood.

In September 1812, the "Pigeon Roost Massacre" occurred near Vienna in Scott County. It was accomplished by Delaware and Shawnee Indians over a personal family feud with the settlers. Their retreat crossed the river at Sparksville. Yellow Beaver led the raids at Pigeon Roost and Leesville. The raiders were chased by a group of 150 mounted riflemen under the command of Major John McCoy.

Part of this group was made up of Washington County militia led by Captain Henry Dawalt. His men included Arthur Parr, Stephen Shipman, John McKnight, Alexander Little, Thomas Thompson, James Thompson, Tart Fordyce, Levi Wright, Noah Wright, John Zink, Daniel Zink, John Thompson, John Dunlap and his two sons, John Curry, James Curry and James Ellison. They were later joined by a party of rangers led by Captain Bigger at Vallonia, before the skirmish near the Haw Patch.

The militia had ridden all night to investigate the rumor of the massacre at Pigeon Roost. When they got close, Arthur Parr let it be known that he thought their chase was a false alarm. Another of the men asked Parr why he thought it was a false alarm and he said, " I smell bread baking and meat frying, and I shall be ready for breakfast when we get to where it is." The frying meat he smelled was the bodies of the settlers roasting in the remains of their cabins and the bread was their corn fields burning. They pursued the fleeing Indians north of Sand Creek in what is now Bartholomew County. In an area of fallen timber known as the Haw Patch, they lost the track of the Indians and turned back. As they came upon a small rise they found the Indians. Captain Dawalt ordered a charge. The stolen horses were loaded with the loot that had been obtained at Pigeon Roost. The Indians cut the packs loose from the horses and tried to get away. In the ensuing skirmish, Thomas Thompson took to a tree and got a good shot off at one of the Indians and wounded him.

The woods was in confusion as both parties scattered and tried to kill the other. Thomas Thompson and John Zink were together. They heard noises in the brush and took cover behind trees. They discovered the Indian, Little Joe Killbuck, standing upon a fallen tree trunk. Both militia men took aim at Killbuck and tried to fire, but their flints locks only snapped. The Indians heard them and gave a heinous yell. Thompson held his position but without a firearm. Zink bent over to recover his flint, but in so doing he exposed his backside from behind the small tree where he was standing. Another Indian, who was hiding behind the tree which Killbuck was standing on took aim on Zink and shot him near the kidney. Zink could not walk and told Thompson to leave him since he was bound to die. Thompson stayed with Zink till dark and then moved him to a dense thicket to hide Zink until he could find the rest of the militia scouts. In the night, Zink heard the Indians hunting for him to scalp and kill him. He pulled himself from sapling to sapling in an attempt to move away from the Indians. By sheer fortitude and will power, Zink moved about 200 yards from where Thompson had left him. Thompson returned the next morning with some of the militia. They made a stretcher to move Zink and took John Zink to Vallonia in that manner. However, Zink died after they arrived at Vallonia, on September 6, 1812. John died at the early age of 21 and was mourned by all his friends and neighbors as a truly brave frontier hero.

Five hundred Indians (Kickapoo and Winnebagos) attacked Fort Harrison near Terre Haute and 500 more (Potawatomi and others) attacked Fort Wayne. Both forts were saved by relief troops from Kentucky. Chief Logan, while spying for General Harrison, said the Indians at Fort Wayne numbered 1,500.

From September 13 to 19, 1812, different detachments of troops destroyed several Indian villages in northern Indiana. On the banks of the Elkhart River, the resident village of the Potawatomi chief, O-ox-see, or Five Medals, was burned by a detachment under Colonel Wells. The Miami town called Little Turtle's Town, on the banks of the Eel River about 18 miles from Fort Wayne, was destroyed by the troops of Colonel Simrall. General Payne's troops destroyed a Miami village at the forks of the Wabash southwest of Fort Wayne. Chief Logan was mortally wounded on November 22, 1812, after Logan had killed the Potawatomi chief Winamac in a skirmish.

Colonel Thomas Campbell led troops on Miami and Potawatomi village destruction actions along the Mississinewa and Wabash rivers in late 1812. The Indians attacked his camp on the night of December 12, 1812. He lost about 40 men that night. The Indians lost about the same. On December 17, Colonel John B. Campbell of the 19th U.S. Infantry found three villages inhabited by Delaware and Miami Indians. He destroyed them and three other villages. As he was preparing to retreat to Ohio, he was attacked by Indians and eight of his men were killed and 42 wounded. His troops took several Indian prisoners. They were of the Munsees, of Silver Heels' band.

Kentucky congressman and militia Major General Samuel Hopkins mounted an unsuccessful search and burn raid along the Tippecanoe and Illinois rivers in the summer of 1812. This was to be against Kickapoo and Peoria villages in Illinois. In the fall he tried again to burn Indian towns along the Wabash, but was ambushed on Wildcat Creek near modern Lafayette.

In June 1813, Colonel Joseph Bartholomew led an expedition of 137 men from Fort Vallonia to attack a Delaware town on the west fork of White River. There they captured an old Indian named Treatway who was a brother to the Delaware chief Buckongahelas. They returned on June 21. Treatway had befriended Daniel Boone when Boone had been captured and adopted into his Indian tribe.

On July 1, 1813, Colonel William Russell led the Seventh U.S. Regiment against Indian villages on the Mississinewa River. Part of the 575 troops were Bartholomew's troops which included Captain Bigger's company. The march was about 250 miles long. In late summer 1813, Colonel Russell took regular and militia troops out from Fort Harrison on a five-hundred-mile sweep of the few remaining hostile Indians in Indiana. He burned their towns, destroyed their crops and confirmed that they had fled the territory. The Indians in Indiana had been subdued.

After the British defeat at the Battle of the Thames in October 1813, some Indians returned to Indiana and did some raiding. These were primarily small bands of less than twenty braves from the Potawatomi and Kickapoo tribes.

Little Turtle later spoke to the United States Congress and to the legislatures of Ohio and Kentucky. One of the main points that he made with each body was "We had better be at war with the white people, for this liquor that they introduce into our country is more to be feared than the gun and tomahawk. More of us have died since the treaty of Greenville than we lost by the years of war before, and it is all owing to the introduction of this liquor among us."

The first recorded gift of liquor to an Indian was by Henry Hudson at Albany, New York. At a September 18, 1609, meeting of Hudson and the Indians, gifts were given by both groups to the other. Hudson invited several chiefs to a cabin. One of Hudson's men brought him a decanter of wine and aqua vitae. Henry took a drink and offered it to the chiefs. One chief sniffed it cautiously. Wiser than they knew, all feared to drink, until one warrior drank the gift. In a short time, he staggered and fell. After a short time, he arose and declared that nothing had ever given him such a feeling of happiness as this drink. Then they all tried it and in the end they were all drunk. Two-hundred-forty years later, many tribes have drunk themselves out of their homeland, prestige and existence. Lockridge said in his *Story of Indiana* that "Investigation showed that where one Indian had been killed in battle, at least ten had been killed in drunken brawls and that numberless squaws and papooses died of starvation because everything went for firewater."

The Moravian missionary to the Indians, Heckwelder, related the following story of an Indian who traded pelts at the Bethlehem, Pennsylvania, mission. "Well, Thomas," said the trader to him, "I believe you have turned Moravian." "Moravian," said the Indian. "What makes you think so?" "Because," replied the other, "you used to come to us, to sell your skins and peltry, and now you trade them away to the Moravians." "So," replied the Indian, "now I understand you well, and I know what you mean to say. Now hear me. See, my friend, when I came to this place with my skins and peltry to trade, the people are kind; they give me plenty of good victuals to eat, and pay me in money, or whatever I want, and no one says a word to me about drinking rum—neither do I ask for it. When I come to your place with my peltry, all call to me, 'Come Thomas—here's a rum, drink—it will not hurt you.' All this is done for the purpose of cheating me. When you have obtained from me all you want, you call me a drunken dog, and kick me out of the room."

Another Indian at Pittsburgh was asked by a white, "Who are you, my friend?" The Indian, who was not too drunk too be ashamed of his situation, said, "My name is Blackfish. At home I am a clever fellow. Here, I am a hog."

Many of the Indians tried to adjust to the white man's ways. The cruelest reality of that adjustment was that the Indians just could not understand the white man's values nor divorce his reliance in his traditional beliefs. There were many instances of helpful kindness going both ways between the whites and the Indians. But there were also many harsh cruelties towards the Indians. The Kickapoo kept their distance from the white men whenever they could and escaped the demoralization of their tribe better than the other tribes that accepted the white man's trade so readily. They were industrious, intelligent and clean in their habits and better armed and clothed than their fellow Indians. They left the area and kept moving away from the influence of the whites as long as they could. In the 1850's, they were allied with the Comanche in west Texas. They were part of the reason that the U.S. Army built forts in that area to control the Indians. South of San Angelo, Texas, there is still a creek known as Kickapoo Creek. Some Kickapoo later migrated into Mexico to avoid contact with the Americans.

Another writer estimated that between 1752 and 1816 a total of 780 whites were murdered by the Indians in 106 separate encounters in Indiana. He further estimated that roughly the same number of Indians met a similar ending. In the 1700's, of 37 military engagements the Indians won 31 and the whites, six. During the 1800's there were 58 separate battles. The Indians won 43 and the white settlers, 15. In eight of the 15 white victories, no Indians were encountered, only empty villages were destroyed.

The Delaware were the first Indian tribe to leave Indiana. They left in accord with a series of treaties that culminated in October 1818, at St. Mary's, Ohio. Only a few who had special treaty rights were allowed to stay in Indiana. The rest crossed the Mississippi at Kaskaskia in October 1820. The Potawatomi, who had come to Indiana around 1670, were forced to leave on what became known as the "Trail of Death" in 1838. Part of the trail that they used, they had given to the United States in 1826; it was called the "Michigan Road." The Delaware had given the trail as a friendly gesture and it was for the sake of "benefit to themselves for traveling and increasing the value of their remaining country." The last to leave were the Miami. Originally, they had owned all of Indiana and half of Ohio. The other Indians had either encroached or been permitted into their territory. They departed for Kansas in 1846. Many of the braves who had terrorized the frontier, when remembering their Indiana homes, cried like children. Some returned to Indiana to visit their old homes into the 1870's. One lone Indian who returned to Montgomery County appeared to local residents to be in shock. To all their questions he could only shrug his shoulders and say, "Big trees all gone." He disappeared as mysteriously as he had appeared. Everything that the Indians had cherished and believed in for a thousand years, all they had valiantly fought for in Indiana, was gone, with no real hope of revival. All the clues found of the Indian society that are hidden in the mist of unrecorded history seem to point to a society in the advanced stages of decline by the time the Europeans started to meet and greet them on their home territory. The Indians decimated each other in the prehistory period and left a disjointed social order to encounter the vigor of European invasion. Abraham Lincoln's famous quote, "A house divided cannot stand" applies to the Indian society in America as well as to the American settlers' later conflict with each other.

The end of the Indians' time in Indiana is truly a sad disaster with enough blame to go around for all involved, both white and Indian.

Chapter 6
Trails of the Old Northwest Territory in Indiana

The history of the trails in southern Indiana, and European use of those trails, dates back to early use by the French after 1680, over three hundred years ago. At the earliest times, the White River water system was on the edge of the colonial French area and about halfway between the influence of New Orleans and Quebec. Very little documentation has been found on southern Indiana (outside of Vincennes) that even hints at what was happening here. The Mississippi, Wabash and the Great Lakes water routes were important to the few French who were in the American Midwest. These routes were key to building a ring to contain the English influence from the east and check the Spanish to the south. But the White River watershed was the outback of the outback.

The Miami Indians never were a "canoe people"; they traveled little by water but were great walkers. They did not use birch bark canoes for two reasons. First, there were few trees available for the type of bark needed for canoes; and secondly, the streams were too rocky and had many snags that would puncture the fragile skin of the canoe. Wooden dugouts served very well for their fishing and hunting needs.

The Delaware Indians who came into this area around 1770 called White River "Wapehani" in their language. The original designation of "white" river is thought to have come from the Miami Indians who named it for the color of the water flowing over some rock ledges in central Indiana on the west fork of the river. In 1799, Moravian missionaries wrote in their diary that they were interested in starting a mission in a Delaware village on the "White Clay River" in Indiana near Muncie. The east fork of the river was known as the Muddy Fork. Higher up the river was called Driftwood.

Two references were found to the "Riviera Blanche" (White River) in reports from the French Fort Ouiatenon. One report stated there was a minor fort on the Riviera Blanche. This may have been the Port Royal trading post near (later) Waverly, Marion County.

The other report, around 1750, stated that the French were encouraging the Indians to kill all the British trappers and hunters found on the Ohio River and White River systems. The French wanted this done to discourage trade between the Indians and the British from the Carolinas.

A memorial (petition) was sent to President Washington on November 20, 1793, from the French citizens of Vincennes. They were petitioning for title to their land around Vincennes and in the document referred to a 1742 grant from the natives to the French and their heirs of "an absolute gift of the lands lying between pointe coupee en haut" (near Merom between Terre Haute and Vincennes) "and the Riviera Blanche" (White River) "below the village."

Local legend and rumor suggests that the Monon Railroad was built roughly on an old Indian trail. This would have been from the Falls of the Ohio to Fort Ouiatenon near Lafayette, Indiana. This "Wea," "Wilderness Trail" or "Old War Path Trail" must have been a minor trail even in the late Indian days. Early maps of the Indiana Territory show trails east (in Jackson County) and west (in Daviess County) to the Wabash River in northern Indiana, but none through Lawrence County. The "Wilderness Trail" started in Clark County and went through New Providence (Borden), Pekin, Salem, Bono, Palestine, Bedford, Harrodsburg, Gosport, Greencastle, Crawfordsville and terminated in Lafayette. The Wilderness Trail was only a horseback and ox cart trail. It was poorly marked and crossed many other Indian trails, as poorly marked as it was. When possible, it followed the creek bottoms or ridge tops to give it the flattest terrain possible to traverse. The actual trail may have changed with the necessity of getting around a local problem, such as a tree fallen over the trail, a gully wash on a hillside, a bog or swampy area in a bottom during the rainy season. The "trail keepers" of that time were the large animals who used the trail and kept the opening wide enough for them to get through. The animals important for this function would have been the buffalo, elk, bear and deer. In many places along the trail there were two different ways to get to the same key crossing point. Both routes were used since there was no improved road or marked path to follow. This could be very confusing if this trail crossed another long distance trail going in another direction that was as poorly marked as the one which was being traveled. It took a skillful guide to know which trail to use in each season. A winter trail that passed through a bottom of rank weed growth might be impassable in summer, while a summer path that traversed over steep rocks might be too slippery with ice in the winter. By today's standards, a poorly kept bridle path would have been the equal to a main highway to the Indians' mode of travel. In short, a long trail between two points may not be recognizable at a specific point along its general path due to the trail moving left or right on any whim or occasion. Today, it would be equally difficult to locate because many trail sections would have been made into farm fields and groomed for many generations to raise crops. Few traces of its original purpose would have been left except in woodlots.

One of the east–west trails in the south central area of Indiana was the Cincinnati Trace, which went from Cincinnati to Salem and on to Vincennes by way of Orleans. (The 1805 trail called Kibby's Trace was farther south.) The need for roads was so keenly felt by the federal government that in 1807 they enacted a law of locating, opening and keeping in repair roads in various counties. Federal funds were used in attempting to cut a route from Vincennes to Cincinnati. The road was called Kibby's Trace and went from the River Falls at Clarksville, Indiana, through the Madison area to Aurora and Cincinnati. In September 1809, Governor Harrison went to a treaty meeting at Fort Wayne by traveling the new road (Kibby's Trace) from Vincennes to North Bend, Ohio, and then to Fort Wayne. It took Harrison two weeks for the entire trip.

The first reference to trail improvements was found in legislation proposed on March 10, 1775. The owners adjacent to the trails were required to clear the brush from the trail across their property and keep a path open at least twenty feet wide. This system did not work well and the trails were let to private companies for toll roads. The founders of the New Albany and Salem Railroad obtained their first right of way by this type of grant in the 1840's.

The Wea or Wilderness Trail was one of the many routes for the early settlers to move to the then current frontier between 1790 and 1820. Many moved every few years down the trail 30 to 60 miles or as far as their legs and animals would hold out. They stopped where they could buy some cheap land or found a plot that was not claimed and took squatter's rights until someone bought it at a registered land sales office. They moved on when a legal buyer showed up or, if they legally owned the property, when they could sell the land, hopefully for a profit. Many of the settlers had possessed three or more homesites in Kentucky before starting on the Indiana trails. They probably possessed three or more homesites in Indiana before moving on. Many left children behind as the children came of age and married fellow travelers, or the families buried members in countless small cemeteries in forgotten pastures and woodlots along the way. Some of the cemeteries have names and are remembered; many are not.

Early Indiana history books shed some interesting light on the travel conditions of southern Indiana. One describes the roads as follows:
The Old Northwest Pioneer Period 1815-1840
"Another important road led from the Falls (New Albany) by way of Salem, Bedford, and Bloomington, one branch going north to the Wabash, and one northeast to Indianapolis."

In Indiana, the road north from the Ohio towards Bloomington was described as follows: "Traveling by land becomes of course, traveling by water, or by both; viz., mud and water. Nor is it possible if one would avoid drowning or suffocation to keep the law and follow the blazed road; but he tacks first to the right and then to the left, often making both losing tacks; and all this, not to find a road but a place where there is no road...so we did enter souse into the most ill-looking, dark morasses, enlivened by streams of purer mud crossing at right angles, and usually much deeper than we cared to discover."

A survey by John McDonald of the "Ten O'Clock Line" in 1810 mentioned several Indian trails that it crossed. This survey defined the northern boundary of Harrison's "New Purchase" that included most of south central and west central Indiana. McDonald mentioned three trails in his survey that may be extensions of old Indian trails located on an early Lawrence County map. McDonald mentioned an Indian trail that he crossed at Gosport. This is thought to be the Wea Trail from the Falls of the Ohio to Ouiatenon.

In the early days of Indiana's history, settlers followed the old Indian trails and paths; or, where these did not exist, they would follow the tracks left by animals. Often the early pioneers blazed their own trails. Stories have been related that the first settlers in some parts had to spend nearly a week to blaze a trail only four or five miles long to get to their land. As time went on these traces, after repeated use, were widened and used as roads. The first settlers usually traveled by foot and packhorse. Their cattle and hogs accompanied them, eating off the land and doing their share in trampling down the brush along the trail. These were soon followed by traveling carts, wagons and sleds. Some of the more important traces of early roads were from Vincennes to Louisville, from Troy to Paoli, from New Albany via Bloomington to Indianapolis, and from Charlestown to Brownstown. The wayfarer traveling through the forest considered himself fortunate if he was not lost more than half of the time. Travelers, in an attempt to avoid the mud holes and newly fallen trees on the roads, would detour among the trees. This left not one but several trails for the next traveler who would have to decide which was the right one.

The trail problems in northern Indiana were different from the problems encountered in southern Indiana. The notes of the early surveyors best describe the conditions they encountered there. Uriah Biggs, in his survey report for Porter County in January 1835, stated, "This township is generally unsusceptible to cultivation. A small portion of the north part only can be cultivated. The Kankakee river is a rather sluggish stream. Its banks very low and lined on each side with a heavy growth of timber, mostly ash, some elm, maple, oak and birch, which grow very tall, and is undergrowth with swamp alder, and wild rose, etc. making an interminable forest which is covered with water during the season. The soil in this forest or swamp is loose yellow sand which renders it almost impracticable to approach the river, only when the swamp is frozen." Jeremiah Smith in his report of Starke County stated, "The upland rolling parts of this township have a loose white sandy soil, in some places so loose that a person will sink an inch or two in walking over it. But little vegetation or undergrowth or shrubbery here. On the parts lower or more level the soil though still sandy assumes a more yellowish and in some places very near black clay. The prairies are either dry, by which I mean such as can be cultivated, or they are wet and marshy.... The soil of the prairie in generally black, but the dry spots are so few and far apart that tilling is out of the question, yet a good part of them are excellent for grazing.... The grass is thickly set and looks like an oat-field just before it heads. In it were a few Indian ponies keeping fat and wallowing in natures choicest luxuries. Some of the prairies are too marshy for grazing, and what use they can be put to, I can't tell. ...The soil is black and rich and would be valuable were it not that it overflows, has bayous through it, or stink holes filled with stagnate water, or black-alder and rose-brier pond or marsh." Later these lands were made subject to Indiana "Barrett's Law" which authorized large sections of land to be drained at government expense and that expense added to the local property owner's tax bill. These lands then became very valuable corn fields. Today, northern Indiana little resembles the marshy and wooded swamp found by the first settlers.

The Daniel Boone Connection

Today, well maintained government highways that get us from one place to another are taken for granted. Two hundred years ago, when Indiana was part of the Northwest Territory, the perceptions were different. The main highways were the water courses and they were, at times, undependable. In the first year of President Adams's administration in 1797, it was decided that a land route needed to be opened from Cincinnati through Vincennes to Fort St. Louis at the mouth of the Missouri River. The land that would later be known as Lawrence County had a minor role in that experiment.

Daniel Boone was ask to survey and open the trail with the assistance of about twelve men. His previous successful opening of the Wilderness Trail in Kentucky was his credentials. The new job would not be easy due to some hostile Indians of the Shawnee, Delaware, Tuckahoe and Piankashaw tribes that lived in the area where the trail was to go through. The opened trail assisted the settlement of the new territory by eastern settlers.

The trail was laid out a little south of what is today the U.S. Highway 50 route. It probably followed the route of earlier Indian trails. Its construction was crude. Trees were marked, or 'blazed,' and brush cut and stacked along the side of trail. Boone's men would scout out the area in front of their current location and decide what was the best viable route west from the point where the road then ended. The trail had some limited use for several years and was locally known as the Cincinnati Trace, Boone Trace or the Upper Trail to Vincennes. The trail crossed the Muscatatuck River at Millport and stayed on the south side of White River, past the community of McKinley. The trail proceeded to what would later be the Lawrence–Orange county line and went west to Hindostan Falls in Martin County, passing a little north of where Orleans was later built. In the Hindostan Falls area, the trail joined the Buffalo Trace from the Falls of the Ohio to Vincennes.

References to that trail exist in several early accounts of south central Indiana documents. In 1817, the Washington County commissioners made reference to "the old state road" and "the Cincinnati Trace." By 1821, parts of that old trail in Washington County were declared as public roads. The 1884 Goodspeed history of Washington, Orange and Lawrence counties made references to the trail. That history stated that the trail had been designated a Federal Road and it existed years before Washington County was formed. The 1884 history mentioned that the boundary between Bono Township of Lawrence County and North East Township of Orange County was the Cincinnati Road.

Mention of the trail was made by President Jefferson in a communication to the Senate and House of Representatives in 1808. "In reference to the CINCINNATI TRACE that had been opened 10 years before and needed to be reclaimed—location which was nearly lost in places with over growth."

Old citizens of Washington County recalled seeing wagons on the road with signs attached reading "Headed for Oregon Trail," "Oklahoma Here We Come," and "Pike's Peak or Bust." While the trail was used for much migration west, its existence today is forgotten. Later land routes roughly followed the original trail route from Cincinnati to St. Louis, including U.S. Highway 50 and the B&O Railroad line. One of the few tangible markings of that trail now is the county line between Lawrence and Orange counties.

Chapter 7
Pioneer Stories

Minute Men of Southern Indiana *or* A Mill and a Fiddle

From the *Corydon Republican*, Corydon, Indiana, November 24, 1955

Editor—On November 7, 1811, the Battle of Tippecanoe was fought and forces under General William Henry Harrison broke the back of the Indian Confederacy that was being formed by Tecumseh.

Harrison County played no small part in that battle. The part played by Spier Spencer and his Yellow Jackets is familiar to all students of Indiana history, but Dr. Howard Byrn, a native of Byrneville, now a practicing physician in New Albany, has written a most interesting side light on the battle few in the county have known.

It was October of the year 1811, and the settlers who had built cabins along the little streams which flow through the hills of southern Indiana into the Ohio were busy cutting corn in their clearings and deadenings, or had already started the winter's campaign against the forest.

Beside a little stream twelve miles northeast of the town of Corydon, which was to be the capital of the state formed a few years later, the wheel of Leason Byrn's mill spun 'round merrily and the saw moved busily up and down as it rasped its way through the huge poplar log.

Leason Byrn, the miller, was of Irish descent, while his wife Anna was of Virginia Dutch stock. They had come to Indiana from North Carolina in 1806, bringing with them a few blacksmith and gunmaker's tools. Being an ingenious man, Leason had built with his own hands the useful little grist and saw mill just mentioned. It soon became a meeting place for the settlers for miles around.

It was something of a social center, too, for while a man was waiting to have his corn ground, he could exchange observations about crops, the weather, and politics with others of similar interests. This opportunity for social refreshment was almost as important as the grinding of the grain to men who lived where, as one had said, a man could hear nobody's dog bark but his own.

On this particular morning a larger number of men than usual had hitched their horses to the trees around the mill and were gathered into a group before the door. Their animated conversation was interrupted by the appearance of the miller, who came out brushing the meal from his hands.

"I hear your brother Temple has come to these parts," said one of the men, as the miller seated himself and felt for his pipe and tobacco.

"And they say he is a right smart of a fiddler," said another. "He'll help liven up things for the young folks a bit, and I wouldn't be above shakin' my feet a little myself if I had some real music."

"I came a thousand miles out here to get away from that Tune, and now the Tune has followed me," said the miller. It was plain from the tone of his voice that he did not entirely approve of his brother's fiddling propensities.

"Well, I guess he brought his rifle too, and he may be able to help with that anyway, if what they are saying about Tecumseh is true," said a tall woodsman, who stood leaning on his own rifle at the edge of the little group.

"Josh is always expectin' to be scalped by Injuns." said another of the group. "What do you think about this war scare, Leason? You know the Injuns about as well as anybody."

The miller smoked a few moments in silence and then said with an air of one accustomed to think carefully on important problems: "I can't say that I have seen anything very suspicious about the Injuns around here, but you can't be sure what they are thinking about. You're not always safe behind a mule even if he don't lay back his ears."

"Tecumseh is a slick one I guess, and he's pretty sure to be plotting some devilment—but I don't think the trouble will start here. The Injuns will begin farther north and west, where the settlements are more scattered. Then if they win out there, the redskins will be down here later."

The miller's duties now called him inside the mill. The conversation continued on the same subject but was again interrupted by the approach of a horseman, who came splashing up the little creek, which here served as a road. It proved to be the miller's son Charles returning from one of the trips to Corydon, which were made at long intervals to secure some article not obtainable at home.

The boy leaped from his horse, and without waiting to be questioned he said, "You men had better be stirring 'round. The Injuns will be on the warpath before you know it. Tecumseh is organizing a league of all the tribes in the west and south, and aims to drive the white men out of all the lands that the Injuns sold a few years ago. Governor Harrison has called out the militia, and Spier Spencer is organizing a company at Corydon. He wants every man he can get and aims to start for Vincennes in a few days."

"I'll go for one," said the man called Josh, and almost instinctively he began to examine his rifle.

"I'll start for Corydon as soon as I get my grist home and mold some bullets," said another.

The group soon broke up, the men riding away one at a time with their sacks in front of them across the backs of their horses and their long rifle in the hollow of their arms.

Later in the evening, when the miller had closed the gate, shutting off the water from the wheel, and had climbed the winding path which led to his cabin on the hill, he found that he had visitors.

Two Indians sat on the bench in front of the house and smoked their pipes as they stolidly awaited his approach. Their presence was no surprise to Leason, for, because of his skill as a blacksmith and gun-making and his well known principles of fair dealing, he was patronized even more by the Indians than by the white men.

These Indians had often visited his shop and were well known to him, but this time their errand was not of the usual nature. They wanted to borrow a small keg which the housewife kept for storing vinegar and which was highly valued because of the scarcity of such vessels.

Leason's thrifty wife, having little confidence in the Indians, had refused to lend the keg without her husband's advice. She told him that if he let the Indians have it, he would never see it again, and although she had not intended this remark to reach their ears, it was evident by the expression on their faces that they understood at least the general significance. However, Leason let them have the keg, and they went away with grunts of satisfaction.

"Get me a bite of bread and meat, mother. I must see what they are up to," said Leason as he went into the house and began to get his rifle and ammunition ready. Before the Indians were out of sight, he was ready to follow them, eating his meager supper as he went.

The Indians were heading in a northeasterly direction. Feeling sure they were making for John Collins' still house, Leason did not try to keep them in sight all the time, but took the trail which he expected them to follow and depended on getting a glimpse of them now and then on the tops of ridges.

They were traveling at a rapid pace, and it was not long till they came down into the small valley where cold water of a little spring flowed over the coiled tube from which trickled a tiny stream of the fiery liquor know as apple-jack. The keg was soon filled and paid for with a valuable fur, and the Indians started to the westward, passing within a few feet of Leason as he crouched under a bush by the trail.

The task of the pursuer now became more difficult, for it was growing dark, and as he had no idea of the destination of the Indians, he had to keep close to them or risk losing sight of them entirely in the gloom of the forest. Soon it grew so dark that in places he could see nothing at all and had to depend on his ears for guidance. In spite of their load the Indians made very little noise and he had to follow them so closely that he was in constant dread of being discovered. Often when a branch snapped beneath his weight or a leaf rustled, he would pause and listen with suspended breath and wildly beating heart.

Once, as they were passing through a particularly dark hollow, he thought he had surely been discovered for, as he listened and strove to pierce the gloom with his eyes, he could hear no sound from the Indians. With rifle ready he waited, expecting every moment to hear the whizing of a tomahawk or knife, or the crack of a rifle.

After a few seconds of breathless suspense that seemed almost like hours, Leason lowered his rifle and heaved a sigh of relief. Far ahead he had heard faint but unmistakable sound of a footstep on a stony ridge. As he hastened forward, he found the cause of his alarm. The Indians had been passing through an open valley where their moccasined feet made absolutely no sound on the damp earth.

After something more than an hour of this trying work, Leason caught sight of fires gleaming through the trees, and knew that the Indians were near their destination. He took his time in approaching the fires, and long before he could see what was going on, he heard the shouts of those at the camp, welcoming the two Indians with the keg.

The place chosen for the encampment was a triangular piece of level ground, where two small streams united to form the creek beside which stood Leason's own mill not more than a mile below. Across the west fork was a bluff of considerable height, and when Leason had made his way to the top of it, he could see clearly what was going on within the circle of fires without himself being seen.

Already the Indians had tapped the keg, and the fiery liquor was rapidly disappearing down a dozen thirsty throats. Soon the squaws piled fresh wood on the fires, making them blaze brightly, and the warriors formed a circle about a post which had been set up in the middle of the open place. Then they began to dance about the post, keeping time to the slow-beating of a drum in the hands of a fantastically decorated medicine man.

Soon the music quickened, and the dancers changed their movements. They went through all the movements of battle, imitating the stealthy advance upon the foe, the shot from ambush and the scalping of the fallen enemy. Then they rushed with loud whoops upon the post and hacked it to pieces with their tomahawks.

Leason watched for some time, while the dance grew more wild and furious as the dancers made frequent trips to the keg. Then he slipped away down the stream and soon reached home, where he found his wife and oldest son anxiously awaiting him. After giving them a brief account of what he had seen and quieting their fears with his assurance that the Indians meant no harm to the settlers of that neighborhood, he threw himself upon the bed, tired out by the unusual exertions of the night.

He was awakened next morning by the barking of his dog, and an instant later his wife came in greatly excited and reported that the Indians were approaching. They proved to be the two who had borrowed the keg, and they were returning it with a large piece of bear meat as pay for its use.

As a further token of his appreciation the Indian known as Eagle Feather pointed at Leason and said, "Good man."

But his companion, remembering Anna's unwillingness to lend the keg, pointed an accusing finger at her and said, "Heap bad squaw."

Then they glided into the forest and were seen no more at that time.

A little later Temple appeared and the two brothers carefully discussed the situation as it was revealed by the reports brought from Corydon by Charles and by the war dance of the Indians the night before.

"I think we ought to go," said Temple. "Folks must stick together in this God-forsaken country, and if we don't teach the redskins a lesson now, there'll be no end of trouble later. I've noticed that it is the one that gets in the first lick that generally wins in a fight. We can protect our homes better by whipping Tecumseh on his own ground than by waiting till he gathers all his men and comes to burn the roofs over our heads."

"I guess you are right," said the older brother as he rose from the bench on which he had been sitting." You go up and see what the Indians are doing while I go down and start the mill. We may hear more news this morning. Abe Walk ought to be getting back from Louisville by this time."

When Leason arrived at the mill, he found several men already there anxious to get their corn ground as soon as possible so they might be ready to join Captain Spier Spencer's company, which according to reports, was to march next day for Vincennes. They wished to leave their families provided for with food during their absence, and their horses staggered under the huge sacks of corn with which they were loaded.

Not long after the miller set the mill going, his brother returned and reported that the Indians had left the encampment and had started off in a northwesterly direction. From this report it seemed clear that they were on their way to join Tecumseh's forces, and the white men now felt sure that the conflict was inevitable.

A short time before noon Abraham Walk rode up to the mill. After greetings had been exchanged, Temple said, "Did you hear anything over the river about Indian trouble, Abe?" "Heard a lot about it and came by on purpose to tell Leason about it. Governor Harrison is afraid the trouble will be serious and he has called for help from the Kentucky Militia. Major Wells is going to bring a force of mounted riflemen, and Fred Geiger is captain of one of the companies. I promised to go with him, and he asked me to get you and Leason to join his company when they come past here. They can't get started for a week or so, and that will give you time to get things ready. Charley can run the mill while you are gone, can't you, Charley?"

"I'll try if Dad says so," said he, "but I would rather go along." "This won't be any work for boys," said Walk. "It is a long way to Vincennes, and it will soon be winter. But I must be going toward home and get busy getting my corn in. There's not much of it anyway, and if the squirrels and coons and wild turkeys have their way in it a few more weeks more, there won't be any. I'll look for both of you when Geiger comes through." As he rode off, the two brothers nodded assent.

On the night of October 28, 1811, the little force of Kentucky riflemen under Major Wells and Captain Funk and Geiger camped near headwaters of the little stream upon which Leason Byrn's mill stood. Here they were joined by the two Byrn brothers and Abraham Walk, who were at once enrolled in Captain Geiger's company. Next morning after hastily disposing of their simple breakfast, the little party of determined men mounted their horses and rode westward along the famous Old Vincennes Trail.

The woods were at their height of their beauty. The dull red of the oak leaves was mingled with the brighter red and yellow of the beech and black walnut. On the ground were the creeping ivy and other plants of many hues, while here and there would appear ginseng stalks conspicuous because of the peculiarly rich golden yellow of its branching stem and the bright red of its seeds.

But the men had little opportunity for musing upon the natural beauties of the region through which they were passing. For the first sixty miles the road ran through a rough and broken country deeply cut by streams and covered with dense forests, which furnished abundant opportunity for ambush. So it was the possibility of lurking Indians rather than the beauties of the scenery which filled the minds of the men as they glanced keenly into the woods along the trail. However, despite their keen lookout not a single Indian was seen during the whole journey.

At the close of the first day's march the party halted in a deep valley where a number of large springs gushed forth from the ground. The old hunters drank eagerly of the water, but most of the others turned up their noses at the smell of it. Only after being assured that it was of great medical value and highly prized by white men and Indian alike could they be persuaded to taste it. One taste was usually enough, and they began to complain loudly of having to depend upon such stuff to quench their thirst. "It might be good enough medicine," said Temple Byrn, "A man can take 'most anything if it is necessary, but we're not sick, and I'd just as lief swallow a rotten egg as that water."

"You'd better get learn to like it same as we did," said Abraham Walk. "You won't get anything else from this on." And he winked slyly at Leason. This report spread rapidly among the men, and the old hunters confirmed it with apparent gravity, exchanging sly winks when unobserved. The disgust of the inexperienced men knew no bounds, said they seemed almost ready to mutiny and return home. Then Captain Geiger, thinking the joke had been carried far enough, pointed out another spring a few yards away, from which pure cold water gushed forth in abundance. The good humor of the men was largely restored, but to the end of the campaign they would grin sheepishly whenever sulphur springs were mentioned.

Late in the afternoon of the second day the party left the hilly country and made rapid progress across the level plain. The rest of the journey to Vincennes was without any unusual incident, and before noon of the fourth day they passed through the quaint old town and turned northward up the Wabash.

In the late afternoon of October 28, they passed a small Indian village situated on a high terrace by the Wabash where the city of Terre Haute now stands. These Indians belonged to one of the friendly tribes and had grown accustomed to the passing of bands of men coming from Vincennes that the squaws hardly looked up from their evening labors as the party rode hastily past. A few miles farther north they came to the fort which the governor had built on a bend of the river and had called by his own name. With the exception of a small garrison the army had already started northward, but the governor was still there anxiously awaiting their arrival. He congratulated Major Wells heartily upon the large force he had brought and told him of his plan, which was to march up the river to the Prophet's town near the mouth of the Tippecanoe and disperse the Indians gathered there, either by treaty or by force.

He was desirous of executing his plan as quickly as possible, not only because of the approach of winter but also because Tecumseh was at this time absent on an expedition among the Southern Indians for the purpose of inducing them to join him against the white settlers. It was well known that his brother, the Prophet, was not nearly so able a leader as Tecumseh himself.

The next day the party overtook the main body, which because of the baggage wagons and the poor roads, was not making very rapid progress. The Byrn brothers and quaintances in the army, expecially Abraham Walk found many acquaintances in the army, especially in Spier Spencer's company, which had been recruited in and near Corydon. It consisted of mounted riflemen, who because of their yellow fringed hunting shirts and the deadly accuracy of their marksmanship were known as Spencer's Yellow Jackets.

On the last day of October the army crossed to the west bank of the river and marched, now accustomed to the dense forests of the eastern part of the state. There was a great deal of discussion as to what caused the country to be treeless and several theories were proposed. "I wouldn't care what made it if I had a few hundred acres of it down home," said Leason, who always had an eye to business. "We'll load up a section or two and take it back with us," said Abe Walk. "It's not good for anything here. A man would freeze to death if he tried to live on it," he added, buttoning up his homespun coat more closely around him as a chilling blast swept across the open plain. "I would lief risk freezing, as starving while I was trying to get some pesky woods cleared," remarked Temple, whose love of the fiddle and dislike for hard manual labor had caused him to make rather slow progress in clearing his farm.

The march was uneventful and no Indians were seen until November 6, when the army was only five or six miles from the town. Then small parties were seen, but they disappeared without attempting to molest the white men. When the whole army had arrived within two miles of the town, the officers were greatly alarmed upon finding themselves without warning in a strip of rough and wooded country where it would have been easy for a small body of Indians to do great damage. General Harrison immediately ordered the formation of the column changed so that the army would be better prepared for an attack, and the advance was continued with extreme caution. "I don't see any use of all this fuss," grumbled one of the Kentuckians, who was riding in front. "We came through hundreds of places just like this." "But we weren't so close to such a hornet's nest as this," answered another. Nothing happened, however, and the little force soon came out upon open ground, where messengers from the town met them with protestations of friendship and urged them not to approach nearer. Many of the officers wished to disregard these messengers and attack the town at once, but Governor Harrison said that his instructions would not admit such a course.

It was arranged that there should be a conference the following day and that no fighting should take place until after that was over. The Indians pointed out a spot a mile from the town suitable for a camp, and after the officers sent to examine it had reported it to be excellent for their purpose, the army advanced and began to make preparations for spending the night. The place chosen for the camp was a low ridge between the banks of Burnett's Creek and the main valley of the Wabash. Toward the left it widened out, but to the right it grew gradually narrow and terminated in an abrupt point. In front toward the south there was a steep descent of about ten feet, at the foot of which a marshy prairie stretched away towards the town. In the rear a somewhat higher bluff bordered the creek which was fringed with willows. The whole right was covered with trees, but there was little underbrush.

In anticipation of a night attack the camp was carefully arranged in the form of an irregular quadrangle suited to the shape of the ridge, the left side being much longer than the right, while the front and rear sides were nearly equal. Regular troops of the United States Army with companies of Indiana Militia were stationed in the front and rear.

Spier Spencer's Yellow Jackets held the right side, which was only about eighty yards long, while the Kentucky riflemen under Geiger and Funk held the left. Their whole force numbered about one thousand men, of whom about four hundred were regulars. The baggage wagons and tents of the officers were in the center.

No breastworks were thrown up because with the small number of axes in the army there had not been more than enough time to secure the necessary firewood. Huge fires were built along the lines both for cooking purposes and to furnish warmth, for the militia had no tents and many men had not even blankets, and the night was cold with intermittent drizzle of rain. There was considerable discussion among the men as to whether or not there would be a battle, and most of them were keenly disappointed at the possibility of a peaceful settlement of the difficulty. This feeling was not due so much to a blood-thirsty desire for fighting as to the firm conviction that there could be no permanent peace with the Indians til they were thoroughly beaten.

After eating their simple supper, most of the men threw themselves upon the ground to sleep, in this instance the military phrase "slept upon their arms" was literally true of the militia, for not only did each man sleep near the place he would occupy in the line in case of attack, but in order to keep the pan of his rifle dry he slept with it under him. Before most of the men of his squad had finished supper, Leason Byrn was stirring 'round, and in a short time with his accustomed ingenuity he had constructed a fairly comfortable shelter of branches, bark, and leaves. His brother, however, was content to throw himself upon a hastily collected pile of leaves and shiver through the night.

About four o'clock next morning, when Governor Harrison was just pulling on his boots preparatory to rousing his men so that they might spend the hours just before dawn in arms, because that was the hour when the Indians usually attacked, he heard a single shot followed by several others at the northeast corner of the camp. The first shot which opened the famous battle of Tippecanoe was fired by Stephen Mars, a corporal in Captain Geiger's company. He was doing sentry duty and was stationed at the corner of the camp where the left of Geiger's line joined at right angles a company of regulars under Captain Bean. As he moved cautiously back and forth, straining his eyes in his effort to pierce the darkness, he thought he saw something moving in the willows which bordered the creek. He dropped upon one knee with rifle poised and waited. Just then the moon struggled through a rift in the clouds, and he saw not ten steps away a dozen dark forms stealing toward him. He raised his rifle and fired; then as the Indians leaped forward, he turned and ran toward the camp. Three or four rifles cracked and the ill-fated corporal fell dead. The Indians dashed past him into the camp, and when the men in that part of the line, aroused by the shots, leaped to their feet, they found the savages already upon them, and a fierce hand-to-hand struggle ensued.

As Leason Byrn sprang from his improvised shelter, a terrifying scene met his gaze. By the faint light of the dying fires he could see men rushing wildly about, while others, already engaged with the enemy, rolled on the ground in a death struggle. He had hardly raised to his feet when two Indians, brandishing their tomahawks and uttering blood-curling yells, rushed upon him. Without waiting to raise his rifle to his shoulder or take aim, he fired at one of his assailants; then leaping backwards, he swung the butt of his gun desperately at the other. The breech of the weapon struck the Indian full upon the side of his head and stretched him senseless beside his companion. Seeing no more Indians near, Leason began to reload his gun, but found that the lock had been broken by the force of the blow rendering the weapon entirely useless for the time at least. Just then Captain Geiger, who had been hurrying about, reforming his broken line, came by, and Leason reported to him the loss of his gun and asked what he should do.

"I have a spare rifle in my tent," answered the captain, and hastened to get it. The tent was only a few steps behind the line, and as they rushed into it, the captain almost fell over an Indian coming out. Before the savage could recover from the shock of the encounter, the captain had thrust his sword through him. As Leason, who still held his damaged rifle, struck at a second Indian, a little behind the first, the savage threw down the saddle bags which he had just split open with his scalping knife and darting under the tent wall, escaped. Securing the rifle, the two men hastened back to the front of the line.

The Indians were now attacking all sides of the camp, and their war whoops, mingled with the rattle of musketry, made a hideous uproar. The fires had been extinguished, but the flashes of the muskets showed clearly the lines of the camp, while all around and appallingly near, the rifles of the Indians like gigantic fireflies lighted up the darkness. Upon hearing the first shots, Governor Harrison had leaped upon his horse and hastened to the point of attack. Finding the men there hard pressed and the line badly broken, he had brought up a company of regulars and another of militia from the center of the rear line, where the attack was not so heavy, to reinforce the companies of Bean and Geiger at the angle. With their support the line was reformed, and the Indians who had broken into camp never got out again.

The Indians had failed in their attempt to scatter the army by the suddenness and force of their attack, and the contest now became a test of endurance and skill, in which because of their organization and discipline the white men had a decided advantage.

Finally daylight came, revealing the strongest body of Indians on the flanks. Spencer's Yellow Jackets on the point of the ridge were having a hard time of it, being exposed to a crossfire from the Indians along the bluffs on both sides. The captain and most of the subordinate officers had been killed while courageously leading their men, but the brave riflemen still held on.

Another company was sent to reinforce them, and then the company of dragoons was ordered to charge the Indians on the left. Major Wells, mistaking the order, led his Kentuckians forward. Dashing from tree to tree, firing whenever they saw an enemy, they soon had the Indians on the run.

During the charge Leason Byrn found himself behind a tree hardly large enough to shelter him, with an Indian behind another a short distance in front of him. As with rifle poised he peered cautiously around the tree trying to get a glimpse of the Indian, a puff of smoke came from behind another tree a little to the left, and he felt a sharp stinging pain in the calf of his left leg. The Indian who had fired the shot, not daring to stop to reload his gun because of the approach of other white men, now broke from his hiding place and started back through the forest. Leason fired at him as he ran and saw him fall forward and lie still. The Indians now broke and fled towards the town; the dragoons pursued them as far across the marshy prairie as they could urge their horses to go.

Being thus relieved of the danger of other bullets, Leason examined the wound in his leg, and finding that it was not serious, he bound it with a strip of bark around it to check the flow of blood and went forward to where the Indian lay. He was not dead, and Leason looked into his upturned face, he was surprised to recognize Eagle Feather, one of the Indians who had borrowed the keg only a few days before. The dying man knew him, and with a strong effort he asked; "Will the gunmaker scalp his red brother?"

"No," answered the other, "but tell me why you attacked your white brothers in the darkness of the night after your chiefs had promised that there would be peace till after the council."

"Elkswatawa, the Prophet," groaned the Indian. "He promise to make the white man's powder sand and make them all sleep. He promise great medicine. He tell us go up close, white man's bullets no hurt. He stay across creek on rock, and make medicine."

The Indian's breathing was now in short gasps, and it was only with great exertion that he could speak. Looking appealingly into the face of the white man and reading there the sign of a true sympathy, he finally asked, "Will the gunmaker hide Eagle Feather's body so others no take scalp?" Leason, mindful of the strong friendship that had once been between them, promised that he would do so, and in a few minutes the Indian was dead. After looking around to see that no white men were near, Leason hastily covered the body with leaves so that it was not easily visible and then started back toward the camp.

He now had an opportunity to think over the events of the night, and the thought of his brother came to him with a sudden pang of anxiety and remorse, because he had neglected so long to look after his safety. Their station in the line had been some distance apart, and he had not seen Temple since the beginning of the battle, though once he had heard his voice raised in shout of triumph at some particularly effective shot. Now when the tense excitement of the battle had somewhat calmed and he had time to think of the many deadly perils of the night's battle, his fears increased greatly.

As he hurried along toward the camp as rapidly as his wounded leg, which was now becoming stiff and sore, would allow, he caught sight of a man at some distance among the trees. Thinking it might be one of the Indians left behind in the flight of the main body, he advanced cautiously. The other did the same, but in a few minutes Leason saw it was a white man, and as they came nearer, to his great relief, he recognized his brother.

His backwoods training, however, prevented any show of feeling, and he merely said as they came within speaking distance of each other, "Is that you, Temple? I was just looking for you." "I was just looking for you, too," answered Temple. "What is the matter with your leg?" "Just a scratch a bullet gave me when I stuck my leg too far 'round a tree a bit ago. It was Eagle Feather who shot me and he's dead now."

When the two brothers reached the camp, they found it in great excitement. Half a hundred men, including many officers, lay dead upon the ground while more than a hundred others had been wounded. Many of the soldiers had been as steady as the regulars during the deadly fighting in the darkness, but now when the strain was relieved, the reaction set in, and the sight of so many dead and wounded men entirely unnerved them.

The day was spent caring for the wounded, burying the dead, and fortifying the camp. Weapons were checked, new supplies of ammunition issued, and the dead or badly wounded officers were replaced. No attempt was made to attack the town, for there were rumors that Tecumseh was approaching with a large body of Indians. Probably the man whose death was most mourned was Captain Spier Spencer.

That night no one slept but though the dogs from the town caused frequent alarm by prowling about the camp no enemy appeared. On the next day a force sent to the town found it deserted and after taking as much corn and beans as they could carry, for the army was now very short of provisions, they set fire to the town and burned it to the ground. On November 9, the wounded were loaded into the twenty-two wagons, and the return march began. Six days later the army reached Fort Harrison, where the wounded, who had suffered untold agonies in the jolting wagons, were made more comfortable in the boats.

The army marched on to Vincennes, where the Kentucky riflemen were mustered out of the service and started at once for their homes. A few days later the little mill on the creek was grinding away with renewed vigor, while from the cabin across the valley came forth the merry notes of the violin.

Tales of Tom Bell

From *The Shelby Sentinel*; May 24, 1882, Shelbyville, Kentucky

Fifty years ago, Tom Bell, an old Revolutionary soldier, was well known by the people about Christiansburg and Pleasureville. His little log cabin was built on Six-mile Creek long before the line was established between the counties of Shelby and Henry, and at a time when he might have claimed any spot of land that his fancy dictated. But Tom Bell was a typical backwoodsman and he located where game and fish were most plentiful. In his little smoky log cabin he reared a large family, but what has become of his posterity I have no means of knowing now.

The writer can remember of seeing Bell, and of hearing him talk of the hardships of the Revolutionary soldiers and of his own individual adventures. He was an Indian fighter, and had many narrow calls for his life, and could tell many interesting stories of adventure. He was no brag like the average backwoods of the times; what he had seen and done did not strike him as being extraordinary, therefore he conversed quite modestly about them. He was a long slender, gaunt old man, and possessed few ideas of civilized life, but he was not without genuine impulse of loyalty to friendship.

After the game that once so abundantly on Six-mile Creek had been destroyed and Bell had grown too old to move to fresh hunting grounds, he eked out but a scanty living to the day of his death, which occurred at a ripe old age. His remains rest near the banks of the stream he loved so well and his grave is only marked by a clump of briars and bushes. Tom Bell, though an Indian fighter, never boasted of his exploits and confessed that he had done some deed in running from the "red devils." A good Indian fighter had to be a good "runner" as well as a good fighter.

He served seven years in the Revolutionary War, half of the time on his own account and the other half as a substitute for a neighbor who had a large and helpless family to support, and who was drafted to his great grief. After Bell's first term had expired and he returned home, he visited his neighbor who had been drafted, and he found him in his field gathering his corn and weeping as he snapped the ears of corn. Bell asked him what was the matter and he told of his distress on account of his helpless family. Bell then and there volunteered to go in his place without compensation whatever. I once hear Bell tell a story of adventure with the "redskins" while he was in the army that seemed to please him very much. They were in camp and news came that "signs of Injuns" had been seen some distance from the camp and a squad, among whom was Bell, was sent out to investigate. They "scouted" two or three miles and found themselves in a skirmish with a band of Indians. The Indians outnumbered the party of soldiers and it became necessary to retreat, which they did "every fellow for himself." Tom Bell discovered that three "big Injuns" had set their hearts on his scalp, and the race was a beautiful one. Bell's gun was empty and he had nothing for it but his legs. It was hot weather and his clothes were ragged, and being pressed to keep out of reach of his savage foes he "stripped himself to his shirt," and ran "like a deer" through the woods in the direction of the camp. He gained on the Indians, and crossing a ravine near the camp he saw water and being nearly famished on account of thirst, he dropped on his knees to quench his thirst when two or three bullets plowed up the water and sand in close proximity to his head. He sprang to his feet unhurt, and in his own words, he made his "shirt tail crack" as he "ran up the hill to the camp." None of his adventures seemed to antimate him like this particular successful race he made in front of the three "big Injuns."

When the writer used to see Bell he was a very old man, and rode a little poverty stricken horse, barely tall enough to keep his rider's unusually long legs from touching the ground. "We boys" regarded the old veteran as a genuine curiosity. But I can remember well that the best people of the times treated Bell with very great respect because of fidelity to his country's cause.

This Tom Bell is also thought to be the one who at Bryan's Station was the rider who rode to Lexington for reinforcements when the Indian seiged the fort there. His service record stated that he had served as a private with Washington at Valley Forge, served at the Battle of Monmouth, and had served on the western front as a dispatch rider.

Micajah Callaway, Indian Fighter

From the *Salem Democrat*, January 19, 1876

Micajah was a remarkable man. He was for many years the companion of Daniel Boone and was with him in many fights with the Indians. Micajah was one of the best scouts and spies. It was related of him that he could walk through the woods, and if your back was turned towards him he would be close to you before you would hear him. He was more than a match for the wily savage, and many a one has been stretched out upon the ground, lifeless, by the unerring bullet from his long rifle. To his death he hated the red skins.

Micajah Callaway was born at Lynchburg, Virginia, about 1755. In 1775 or '6, he came to Kentucky, where he became a Boone companion who was a great scout, hunter, and Indian hater. In 1777, the people of Boonesborough were suffering a great deal for want of salt. The labor and risk was too great to any longer pack it over the mountains on horseback. That was the only way they could obtain large quantities of this necessity of life, which the wild forest wilderness did not furnish. So it was arranged that Boone with thirty men should go to the Lower Blue Licks on Licking River, and boil down the stream's water and obtain a type of mineral salt. Of this number were Micajah Callaway and Flounders Callaway. They set out on New Year's day, 1778. Boone was the guide, hunter, and scout. By the 7th of February they had salt enough to send a supply to the station, and sent three of their men with it while the rest worked on. On this same day, while Boone was out hunting, he was captured by two Canadians and one hundred Shawnee Indians. Boone, finding that he could not warn his companions at the Lick so they could escape, set about making terms for them on their behalf, and finally persuaded his men by signs and gestures to surrender.

Callaway said, in after years, that if they had the least idea of what they were to suffer, they would have fought until the last man was killed. Many of these men were taken to Detroit, Mich., and delivered over to Gov. Hamilton, the British commander of the Northwest. Many were put to the torture; some were killed and scalped by the wayside; but Callaway was retained in Ohio, at what was called the Chilicothi towns. He was compelled to subsist on fish, which he had to catch himself, for three months. All this time he had no salt. Once, he said, that he got a piece of a duck's leg that had been oiled in corn, but the Indians took particular pains to see that he got no corn. His brother, James Callaway, was also a prisoner, but he and Boone escaped at different periods in the spring and summer of 1778. James wandered in the wilderness for twenty-seven days, his only food was frogs which he caught. Micajah has often related to his family and neighbors how, during the period of five years and five months that he was a prisoner with the Indians, he saw the whites tortured; and how he was compelled to sit by and witness it all. The warriors and squaws beat him with their fists and sticks; and how after scalping a victim, the red devils would dash the bloody scalp into his face, and tell him that if he attempted to escape they would serve him the same way. He saw fifteen white prisoners put to the torture while he was with them; and did not recollect how many he had seen tomahawked and scalped.

He well knew the renegade, Simon Girty, and told how Girty used to abuse him, and all white prisoners, and then laugh and scoff at their miseries while the savages tortured them. Callaway was in the war of the revolution; and for the services there rendered, he drew a pension. After peace was declared in 1783 (probably about 1786), Simon Girty went to Kentucky and settled there. Callaway came across him one day at a gathering at some settlement, and told Girty he would kill him for his many acts of barbarity and murder that he had instigated the savages to commit, even if he had done no murder himself. Girty, desperado that he was, begged Callaway to spare his life, which Callaway agreed to do upon the condition that if he (Girty) should ever be in a settlement town or gathering of the settlers, and Callaway came there, Girty was to leave at once and not say a word. Girty readily assented and hastily departed. Callaway traveled around considerably just to see Girty make tracks at his coming. Callaway only wished Girty would stand his ground, in order that he might avenge the terrible wrongs of Girty to his former prisoners. The whole country found out about how Girty had to move when Callaway came about; and he was taunted and jeered wherever he went, until finally he abandoned Kentucky.

Callaway said the Indians never tied him, but adopted an equally safe manner to keep him securely. It was really novel and safe way. The Indians would cut down a hickory sapling, and split it up from the butt some three feet. At about two feet from the end, they would hollow out a round plane large enough for the ankle to turn easily in. They would then sharpen the lower end, and then cut off about five feet of a sapling. They would then open the split end, make the prisoner lay his ankle in, and then drive the sharp end in the ground until the ankle was even with the top of the ground. In this manner they were kept every night and there was no chance of escape at all. Callaway resided in Kentucky after his release from the Indians and the way he got away was as follows: After the war, there was to be an exchange of prisoners at the Falls of Ohio, and Callaway was the interpreter. After the exchange was made, he refused to go back, although not exchanged himself. The savages made great offers to induce him to return, but he refused and went up to Kentucky to his old home and friends, where he resided until 1803. During this time, 1796, he married a woman by the name of Mary Arnold.

From the *Salem Democrat*, January 26, 1876

In 1803, Micajah Callaway and others emigrated to Missouri—Daniel Boone had already preceded them. The company went on horseback, and packed their few goods on pack horses. They crossed the Ohio at Cincinnati, and took what was known as Boone's track, being a direct west course, as near as they could for the settlement. That trace ran through this county, on the ridge between the old Henry Lick place and Millport. We do not know the precise location of it. The settlement was about twenty miles above St. Louis, and some two miles back from the river. Here Callaway's wife and infant daughter sickened and died of the malarial fever. Callaway said that he had as many as three severe chills inside of twenty-four hours. He told his companion settlers that they might stay there if they liked, but as for him, he was going to hunt some healthier locality. So catching his horse, he made a pannier like unto a pair of saddle bags, which he put over the pack saddle, and putting his son James in one end, and Edmund in the other, and a few necessary articles on the saddle, he shouldered his rifle and started alone to travel about four hundred miles through the wilderness, where the wild savage barbarian roamed at will. But he safely made the trip to Kentucky, subsisting himself and children on the way by the game that he caught.

In 1794, when General Anty. Wayne marched against the Indians through Ohio and the northern part of Indiana, Callaway was his principle scout and spy. He was well acquainted with the whole country. When far to the north, in Ohio, near a branch of the Miami, the scout observed on the far side a couple of Indians. He knew by their actions that many more must be there, and that no doubt an ambush was prepared. He hastened back to inform the officer of the advance guard, but when he came up in view, he accused Callaway of having the "Shawnee fever," which meant that he smelt danger where there was none. The scout told him that if he crossed his men would catch worse than the "Shawnee fever." But the officer, being headstrong, did not take the warning nor wait for the commanding officer to come up, but plunged into and across the stream. About one hundred yards from the shore was a rise of ground which was bare, and upon this the officer halted his men. No Indians were to be seen. Soon the men had broken ranks and were scattered, when all at once a terrific volley of firearms burst upon them from all sides. The Indians sprang from their coverts, and with wild yells, rushed upon the soldiers. Many were killed and wounded, and the balance fled, panic stricken, back to the main body. The officer in charge was severely wounded, but he never accused Callaway of having the "Shawnee fever" again.

There is one incident connected with the early life of Micajah Callaway that must not be passed over unnoted. One hundred years ago last July, Betsey Callaway, her sister Frances, and Jemima Boone, a daughter of Daniel Boone, were outside of the fort at Boonesborough, in a canoe on the Kentucky river. Betsey was sixteen and the other two about fourteen years of age. They were in plain sight of the fort at Boonesborough. It was late in the afternoon, and they had been carelessly paddling in a canoe. On the opposite bank the brush and trees were thick, and came down to the water, while the canoe, floating with the current, drifted near the opposite shore. Five stout Indians had been lying there concealed, one of whom, as noiselessly and stealthily as a serpent, crawled down the bank until he reached the rope attached to the canoe, and turned it up the stream. He had no sooner seized it and started when Betsey gave him a terrific blow on the head with the edge of the paddle, nearly scalping him. With an Ugh! he fell, when the others seized it, and soon the girls were out of sight of the fort. The loud shouts of the girls were heard at the fort, but too late for their rescue. The canoe, the only means of crossing was on the opposite shore, and none dared to swim, for they believed that a large body of savages were concealed in the brush. These Callaway girls were the daughters of Richard Callaway and cousins of Micajah. Richard, Micajah, and Boone were all absent, and it was after night before they returned, and before the arrangements for the pursuit were completed.

Among those in pursuit was a Col. Floyd, and as he gives in one of his memories some account of the chase and rescue, we have taken some of our information from them. Next morning, by daylight, the Callaways, Boone, Floyd, and others were on the track, but the Indians had done their best to obliterate their trail. The girls had, however, every once in a while, torn a strip from their aprons and dropped along to show their pursuers and rescuers the route they had gone. When they had traveled about thirty miles the Indians discovered their trick, and under threats compelled them to stop it. After this, whenever they got a chance, they would bend or break a twig, as a guide to the unerring woodsmen. When they had gone about fifty miles the Indians became less watchful, but at night when they did not tie or bind them, they compelled each girl to lie down with an Indian on his blanket, when he would put one of his legs across them. This was all the violence offered them. The Callaways, Boone, and others were closely following the trail, and supposed they would soon overtake them.

From the *Salem Democrat*, February 2, 1876

After the scouts had been out two days and nights, on the morning of the third day, they had gone but a few miles when they struck a buffalo path, and there Callaway said they found their track plain. They pursued on as the morning sun rose higher in the heavens, well knowing that the tracks had not long been made. After going about ten miles, they overtook them just as the Indians were kindling a fire to cook their breakfast. Their study then was, how to get the prisoners, without giving the Indians time to murder them after they discovered their pursuers, for that was the invariable custom of the savages to murder all their prisoners rather than they should be retaken. The Indians discovered their pursuers, and the scouts had no time to arrange the details. Four of them fired, and all rushed on the Indians, by which they were prevented from murdering their prisoners, and from carrying anything away. Three of them got away but Callaway was certain that two of the three were badly wounded. The other two had gone to the happy hunting grounds. The place was covered thick with cane, and they were so elated at the rescue of the girls, that they did not search further for the wounded Indians who fled, leaving moccasins and everything but an old shot gun, which they got away with. A son of Daniel Boone afterwards married Betsey Callaway.

As we have said, Micajah Callaway settled in this county in 1810 and lived here until he died. We have heretofore given several incidents of his life. He lived where he settled, until he died in 1840 at the advanced age of 94 years. His wife survived him and died in 1864. Their son, John H. Callaway, now resides at the old homestead. Micajah Callaway was a man of strong likes and dislikes. If a man once insulted him or tried to take the advantage of him, he never forgot it, and he never liked such an one thereafter, and wanted little to do with him. He had an inveterate hatred for the savages and also for those who would not help to chastise and punish them in the same manner they served on the whites. We do not know that we can close this sketch of this old pioneer better than by giving a short statement of the manner the Indians so inhumanely tortured their victims at the stake. He told it to his children so often, that it is seared into their very brains and never will be forgotten. We will give one which is only a sample of the many that he was compelled to witness.

It was in 1779 that the Indians had captured an officer of the militia, and if there was one torture worse than other than savage fiendishness could invent, it was applied to the officer, for they never escaped the most terrible of deaths. Callaway speaks of this one as taking place on 11 June 1782. There was a Captain Pipe there at the time as well as Simon Girty. The prisoner Captain William Crawford's face was painted black by Captain Pipe, and while doing so he told him that he would have him shaved. Other prisoners had been taken, and as they were marched along, they saw several dead bodies and all were scalped. They had been tomahawked. When they got within a half mile of where the execution took place, they overtook five more prisoners and they were all made to sit on the ground. The squaws and boys fell upon the five, and tomahawked and scalped them. There was a man named McKinley among the prisoners, and an old squaw cut his head off, and the Indians kicked it about the ground. Nearly every Indian that they met or passed struck the prisoners. The prisoners were taken near the five and Crawford was stripped naked, and then they made him sit down and they beat him with their fists and sticks. They then tied a rope to the foot of a post about fifteen feet high, bound his hands behind him and fastened the rope to the ligature between his wrists.

The rope was long enough for him to sit down or walk around the post once or twice, and back the same way. He called to Girty and asked if they were going to burn him. Girty replied yes. The Captain said he would take it all "patiently." Then Capt. Pipe made a speech in Indian tongue to about a hundred men, women, and children. And when he was done, they all yelled assent. The Indian men then took up their guns and shot powder into the Captain's body from his feet to his neck. There was from seventy to eighty loads fired into his naked body. They then cut off his ears, pulled his toe nails out by the roots, which he bore with great firmness. They had slapped fresh scalps in the faces of the other prisoners to vary their pastime. The fire was six to seven yards from the post to which the Captain was bound and was made out of small hickory poles, burnt quite through in the middle, each end of the poles running about six feet in length. Three or four Indians would by turns take up one of the burning pieces and apply it to the Captain's naked body, already burnt black with powder. Then his tormentors would present themselves on every side of him and apply burning fagots and poles. Some of the squaws would take broad boards, upon which they would get hot ashes and live coals and throw on him, so he soon had nothing but hot ashes and live coals to stand or walk on. During the torture he begged Girty to shoot him. Girty replied that he had no gun and laughed heartily. The Captain bore all his torments with great fortitude. For about five hours were they thus torturing him, Callaway an unwilling spectator of it all. Finally, the Captain being almost exhausted, lay down on his face. They then scalped him and dashed the scalp in Callaway's eyes, and said, "That is your great captain."

An old squaw whose appearance everyway answered the idea the people entertain of the Devil, got a board, took a parcel of coals and ashes, put them on his back after he had been scalped; he then raised himself to his feet and began to walk around the post; they then applied the burning sticks again, but he seemed more insensible to pain than before. They then mutilated his person and continued playing their burning sticks again, until he fainted away. They then beat him. When he finally revived, they untied him and laid him across the slow fire, one Indian holding his head down and others his feet. In this way they tortured him to death. Such were the scenes that Micajah Callaway witnessed.

When we think that for five years and five months, he was compelled to witness such scenes and when we remember that the renegade Simon Girty gloated over the torture and misery of his own race, we almost wonder that Callaway did not take his life at the first opportunity. We don't know but that Girty ought to have been tortured in the same manner that his victims were. When we think of all these things, and thousands of others, is it any wonder that the frontiersman and pioneer hates the red savage. We do not wonder he gives him a bullet every chance he gets, and only wishes it were twenty instead of one.

Chapter 8
Early Leaders in Indiana History

James Bigger: Ranger Captain

James Bigger and his life seem to be typical of the bravado and courage of the early pioneers of the Indiana soil. The first mention of Captain Bigger finds him in charge of militia men at Fort Maxwell on Lost River in northeastern Orange County, Indiana, in 1810. He was captain of a rifle company in the 2nd Regiment of Harrison's Army and his company of "Bigger's Rifles" were involved in the Battle of Tippecanoe in November 1811; however, on the day of the battle it may have been under the command of another officer, Reid.

Later, in 1812, James Bigger was in the Charlestown area in Clark County organizing a company of Rangers to help protect the citizens from Indian raids on their isolated cabins. The Rangers were halfway between U.S. Army active duty status and Citizen Militia status. His patrols ranged over most of the south central area of what would become "The Hoosier State." In the later historical remembrances of the men who served with him much mention is made of chasing and killing Indians in the act of terrorizing local settlers in their cabins between the years of 1812 and 1815.

Mention is made of the many patrols sent out from Fort Vallonia to the western Indiana area Indian villages on the west fork of White River and up the east fork of White River to the Muncie area in pursuit of Indians, as well as patrol actions in Washington, Harrison, Orange and Knox counties in southern Indiana. While stationed at Vallonia, Captain Bigger taught the first school class in Jackson County in 1812-1813.

Bigger's First Sergeant in the Rangers company was John Ketcham. Ketcham was influential in founding Brownstown, Indiana, and donating land for the Jackson County courthouse. Brownstown is about three miles northeast of Fort Vallonia. Later, when Bigger moved to the Bloomington, Indiana, area, John Ketcham also moved to nearby Ellettsville. Ketcham stayed there the rest of his life. John Ketcham and Jack Storm were the reason the creek running through Elletsville was named "Jack's Defeat Creek," which it is still called today. They both were trying to cross the unnamed creek while on military maneuvers with General Tipton and Captain Bean. The creek was rain-swollen and their horses became mired and could not get free. Their fellow soldiers came to their rescue, and since the creek was unnamed they decided to call it "Jack's Defeat."

Early trails and maps of Indiana Territory credit a trail named for Bigger that went north from White River in Lawrence County to Bigger's Trading Post in the southwestern part of what would be Monroe County. The map puts this trading post on a ridge between Clear Creek and Indian Creek near Kirksville or the Victor Oolitic Stone Company. The road that traverses the Clear Creek valley at that point is still called Ketcham Road. Bigger's trail went east of Fayetteville about a mile and through Springville to its terminal point at the trading post. It is assumed the trading post was active about 1815.

In Monroe County history, James Bigger was listed as the first County Lister in 1818. The history further stated that he had land in Section 35 of Bean Blossom Township. This location was one township north of the trading post location. Both locations seem to have been on ridge tops. It is deduced that James was of a personality that always wanted to be involved on the forefront of frontier activity. His reputation and specialty seemed to be in hunting and crowding the Indians as much as he could. In 1818, he was appointed to a political position in Monroe County only to be relieved of that position a short time later. By 1822, he was appointed as the first Sheriff of Morgan County. When the town of Spencer was first laid out and the lots auctioned off, James Bigger was the auctioneer.

Within a few years, James Bigger had moved on to new frontiers in Illinois. He is buried north of Bloomington, Illinois, in the Clarksville Cemetery. He is buried close to his old friend and militia commander General Bartholomew in McLean County, Illinois, in the now vanished community of Clarksville.

William Bigger was also in the Bloomington area at the same time James was there. Samuel Bigger was later Governor of Indiana. While the Bigger family was typical of the early families who were just doing what they thought needed to be done on a daily basis to exist, they left an indelible influence on Indiana's development.

Henry Dawalt: Frontier Pioneer and Militia Captain

Born to German parents in Hanover, Pennsylvania, on January 1, 1774, Henry Dawalt moved to Jonesborough, Tennessee, in 1795 and married Elizabeth Gross. Later he moved to the Royce's Fork of Blue River in Washington County, Indiana, in 1809. That land was later patented in March of 1814. Henry bought venison and bear meat from the Indians of his neighborhood. He was well acquainted with Old Ox, Joe Killbuck and McCullough, all active and infamous Indian neighbors of his day. Dawalt was a Captain of a frontier military unit and very active in most of the raids and chases of the Indians during the troubles of the War of 1812 in southern Indiana area. Dawalt led the chase party who pursued the Indians who had committed the Pigeon Roost Massacre in Scott County. The group chased the Indians to "the Haw Patch" on Sand Creek in Bartholomew County where they charged and routed the Indian raiders. The Indians still had their loot from the cabins of the Pigeon Roost community. He also led a party of settlers in the chase of the Indians who murdered the Solidad brothers and another chase of the Indians who stole Jimmy Hensley and Johnny Menaugh in 1812.

Silas McCullough: Scout, Squawman, Preacher

In June 1806, Silas McCullough and family settled near Aquilla Rodgers at the Driftwood Lake area of Mill Creek in Jackson County. The area was not plotted until 1815. Some Indians were occasionally living at the old French trading post at Vallonia. Silas had married the daughter of the Indian Chief, Old Ox, who camped in Gibson Township, Washington County. McCullough had been prospecting and hunting in the general area when he came down with a fever and rheumatism. Old Ox's daughter nursed him back to health and claimed him as hers. They had a son named Sammy.

McCullough spent some of his time at Beck's Mill, living with the Indians there and hunting with them and the Becks. McCullough became a friend of Joe Killbuck, a Delaware Indian reputed to have shot John Zink (among many of Joe's scrapes with the troublesome white settlers), and brother-in-law to Low Head, an Indian who did not get along with the invading whites in *his* land. Joe, Low Head and their relatives were the reason for many of the early forts in Washington County to be built. These Delaware Indians were reported to desire to trade bear meat and skins for whiteman's goods one day, and the next day terrorize the same neighbors by stealing horses, killing stock and waylaying travelers. McCullough is reported to have ventured on all the scouts and hunts with Major Beck. He also functioned as a chief in the Indian councils and was a prominent speaker who carried influence in the tribe's decisions. He also was a preacher to the white settlers, and married some of the young white couples in the neighborhood until of 1814.

McCullough was reported to have been a scout for Harmar on his disastrous march in Ohio in 1790. During the campaign of General Harrison to Tippecanoe from September 18 through November 12, 1811, Silas was listed as a private in the company of Toussany Dubois's spies. The duties of this company were to scout and guide the army up the Wabash from Vincennes. He was also listed as a private in David Holt's Company of Infantry, commanded by Colonel John Miller from July 14, 1814, to October 31, 1814.

After the murder of Hinton at the Cherry Bottoms near Brownstown on April 7, 1812, notice of the murder was sent to the militia leaders. A Cincinnati newspaper of the time stated the murder happened at the "French Store" on White River. Silas McCullough played an important part by telling the probable offending Indians to leave the area before committing another murder. John Ketcham said that the morning after Hinton's murder, three Delaware Indians with guns pushed open his cabin door and forced their way in. Ketcham asked them to be seated and stack their rifles in the corner. Upon his inspection of the rifles, he found them primed and ready to fire. Apparently the Indians were known to Ketcham since they calmly discussed the Hinton murder. The Indians said it was done by Winnebagos. John asked the three to go with him to retrieve Hinton's body. Initially the Indians complied and started to the murder scene with Ketcham. They had gone about a mile when the Indians refused to go further and said "We no go, make white man heap mad." They returned to the cabin. On their return, the Indians retrieved some furs they had cached in the brush near the cabin and stated that their only purpose to come to visit Ketcham was to trade their furs with him.

Just as they returned to the cabin, Silas McCullough and another white man arrived at the cabin. Silas told the Indians to immediately leave or "every devil of them should be killed." Captain Dawalt and his militia were getting organized to pursue the Indians who had recently stolen children and killed men in that neighborhood. The Indians returned to their camp and moved out in such a great haste that they left some items of great value behind. It is unknown if the Indians were afraid of Silas or just his "friendly" message. John Ketcham's family thought he had escaped a fate similar to the Solidad brothers, whom the Indians had murdered only a few miles from the Ketcham cabin. Daniel Solidad lived in Orange County. Solidad had fought at the Battle of Tippecanoe the previous fall and openly bragged about killing and scalping several Indians. Daniel's brother, Jacob Solidad, was also hunted down by the Indians and killed for his part at the battle. The main body of the Indians was trailed into Monroe County to Bean Blossom Creek but the posse turned back at that point.

Ten days later, two Indians (Salt Peter and Peter Vanvacter) came from the Delaware town under a flag of truce with a message from the Indian agent that said the murder had been done by Kickapoo Indians that had come to their village with Hinton's stolen horses.

John L. Menaugh: Boy of the Frontier

John Menaugh was the son of Thomas Menaugh, who emigrated from Ireland with his parents to Uniontown, Pennsylvania. After Menaugh grew up he moved to Charleston (West Virginia) where he served a seven-year apprenticeship in the trade of a hatter. Working his trade, he moved to Kentucky where Johnny was born in 1806. The Menaugh and Hensley families moved to the Salem area together, where Johnny Menaugh and Jimmy Hensley were playmates. Among their friends was Sammy McCullough. Sammy's father, Silas, was a noted Indian scout for General Harmar on his raid of the Mississinaw. His mother was the daughter of the Indian chief Old Ox. The three boys played together most of the time.

In the spring of 1812, Old Ox's wife (Sammy's grandmother) invited Johnny and Jimmy to come to Sammy's home to play and told Mrs. Menaugh and Mrs. Hensley that the boys would come home later. Since they had played with Sammy before, the mothers agreed. However, the boys did not return home when expected. The parents went to Sammy's home to find out what was the matter and found the place deserted. The Indians had left and taken Johnny and Jimmy with them. The men of the neighborhood became alarmed and formed a search party to locate the boys, but they were not found. Two mothers were now grieving the loss of their loved sons to an unknown fate.

Later it was learned that the Indians had split into two groups. The smaller group had taken Jimmy and Johnny north from Salem to the Muscatatuck River near Vallonia and hidden. Later they made their way to the Indian villages near where Lafayette, Indiana, is now. Somewhere along the trail, they built a campfire for the night and placed Jimmy and Johnny near the fire to sleep, with the fire keeping them safe from the wolves and cougars. During the night, while the boys were asleep, the robe one of them was bundled up in caught fire from an ember of the fire. He was burned so badly that the Indians did not think he could safely travel with them, so they killed him and took his scalp and left his body for the animals of the forest to devour. The other boy was raised by the Indians as one of their own. However, at a later time, the boy was one of several prisoners bought from the Indians at Fort Vincennes. The Hensley and Menaugh families heard of the boy at Vincennes who matched the description of their sons. A man was sent to Vincennes by the old Indian trail from Cincinnati to St. Louis to fetch the boy home.

When he returned to Salem, both mothers claimed the boy as their son. There was no consoling either mother that her son was really dead. The community appointed a committee to decide whose boy he was. Andrew Pitts, Samuel Hicks and Colonel Henry Dawalt were chosen. After much deliberation, they could not agree on who the boy was. Henry Dawalt thought Betsy Hensley was the mother. Samuel Hicks thought Polly Menaugh was, while Andrew Pitts thought the boy was Sammy, the half-breed McCullough boy.

A forth man, Jesse Spurgeon, was added to the committee. He found "that the disputed child was of right, Betsy Hensley's but, that there was some doubt about it, he thought that it would be better to award him to both, and let Betsy keep him one half of the time and Polly the other half and if Betsy should outlive Polly, he was to be Betsy's and go by her name but if Polly should outlive Betsy, then he was to belong to Polly and go by her name."

Jimmy Hensley, Johnny Menaugh, or Sammy McCullough was raised by both families as their son until Mrs. Hensley died. Later the Menaughs moved to northern

Indiana where Polly died at Delphi, Indiana, in 1844. Thomas Menaugh died at Kokomo in 1848.

The boy lived the rest of his life as John L. Menaugh in Salem, Indiana.

Later in adult life, John was a leading citizen of Salem, very active in politics and practiced the trade of hatter. In some of his later correspondence, he signed his name as "Old Ox" in honor of his Indian stepmother (or grandmother) who had stolen him as a boy.

Colonel John L. Menaugh served Salem as deputy sheriff from 1842 to 1844: as Sheriff from 1844 to 1848: as a member of the Indiana State House of Representatives in 1849: as County Treasurer from 1850 to 1856: and as Postmaster from 1867 to 1869.

Colonel Menaugh was a man loved and respected in Salem. But, in truth, who was he? JIMMY, JOHNNY, or SAMMY? It's a mystery to this day.

Solidad Brothers: Victims of Revenge

Daniel and Jacob Solidad were veterans of the Battle of Tippecanoe. Both were proud of their hand-to-hand combat with the Indians during the battle where they took several Indian lives. During the winter after the battle, they were peacefully working for settlers near the Buffalo Bottoms area of White River in Washington County. The Indians had made winter camp north of the river and were aware of the brothers' location and targeted them for revenge murders for their killings of the Indian braves.

On the same early spring day, both of the brothers were out hunting lost horses for the different men they were helping. While they were in separate townships, both were about four miles south of White River The Indians lay in ambush in the woods and Daniel and Jacob were killed in a similar manner, while hunting the lost horses.

Daniel and his employer Ellison had found some of the horses and Ellison had returned to his farm with them while Daniel continued to hunt for the rest of the herd. When he did not return, Ellison returned to the dense grove of timber where he had left Daniel and found his body, shot, tomahawked and scalped.

On the same day at about the same time, Jacob was also killed while hunting for horses that belonged to his friend Richard Newkirk They were fired upon and both wounded. Newkirk was slightly hurt and got away but Jacob was more severely wounded and did not escape. He was later found among bloody leaves and boughs and shreds of savage apparel. It was evident that he fought bravely for his life but had lost. His body had been stabbed in several places, tomahawked and scalped.

The slayers of the two men were never overtaken but thought to afterwards have fought with Tecumseh at the Battle of the Thames in Canada, and hopefully were among the Indians killed by the Kentucky long rifles.

George Croghan: Hero of the War of 1812

George Croghan was the son of George Rogers Clark's sister, a boy of the frontier who was anxious and willing to build his future on the challenges of his day. He became a fine leader of Kentucky and built part of his reputation in the greater Lawrence County area in the days when it was wild and untamed.

After the meeting of General William Henry Harrison and Tecumseh at Vincennes in the summer of 1811, Harrison went to the Falls of the Ohio and organized a pressure and pursuit campaign on the Indians of southern Indiana. He charged the Kentucky Rangers with the responsibility to carry out his policy. Some of them were under the direction of Croghan. The encounter of the Kentucky Rangers and the Mohican Indians of Clear Creek was reported in the *Bloomington Evening World* newspaper—the October 10 and October 16, 1900, issues.

The issue stated that Major Croghan had set up a fort at Fort Ritner in August 1811. He had been informed of hostile Indian activity at the mouth of Clear Creek and Salt Creek. Tecumseh had been involved in a meeting with the Mohicans in preparation for activity that would lead up to the War of 1812. Croghan sent Captain James Montgomery, Sergeant Thomas Frisbee, Corporal P. Lowther, Privates T. Grimes, E. Noel, C. Malott, T. Buskirk, Asa Thornton, B. Woodward, and R. Taylor, and guides David McHolland and John Ros Neagy (Indian). They engaged the Clear Creek Indians and Captain Montgomery was killed. Ros Neagy went to Fort Ritner for assistance and Croghan and his 250 men arrived on the scene. Twenty-two soldiers were killed in the ensuing battle that completely subdued the hostile Indians.

Later in the War of 1812, Croghan and his Kentucky men were famous for battles and maneuvers around Sandusky, Ohio, and up to Detroit, Michigan.

John Tipton: From Militia Private to U.S. Senator

John Shields Tipton moved to Harrison County at age 17 from Sevier County, Tennessee. He enlisted in Spier Spencer's company called Yellow Jackets. With the death of Spencer in 1811 at the Battle of Tippecanoe, Tipton stepped in and took command of the unit and preformed commendably. Due to his leadership, he was promoted to Major in 1813 and had command of two companies of Indiana Rangers at Fort Vallonia during the War of 1812.

He served as a member of the Indiana State House of Representatives from 1819 to 1823. During this time, he founded the town of Columbus, Indiana, originally known as Tiptonia, and he participated in commissions to establish a new state capital for Indiana and to set the boundaries between Indiana and Illinois. In 1823, he became the United States Indian agent for the Potawatomi and Miami tribes. In 1831, Tipton was elected by the state legislature to a seat in the United States Senate from Indiana. He was a member of the United States Democratic Party and a strong supporter of Andrew Jackson. He served as chairman of the committees on roads and canals and Native American affairs from 1837 to 1839. In 1838, at the behest of Indiana Governor David Wallace, Tipton was responsible for rounding up 859 uncooperative Potawatomi and forcibly moving them to Kansas in what became known as the Potawatomi Trail of Death. Tipton County and the town of Tipton, Indiana, were named for John Tipton. His death came in 1839.

Joseph Bartholomew: Military Hero

Joseph Bartholomew was born in New Jersey, March 15, 1766. When he was two years old, his family moved to Laurel Hill, Pennsylvania. Though he was only 10 years old at the outbreak of the Revolutionary War, he joined the local militia and helped defend against Native American tribes who were raiding the Pennsylvania frontier.

In 1788, the Bartholomews moved to northern Kentucky, near present-day Louisville, where he remained active in the local militia and engaged in numerous skirmishes with Native Americans. During Little Turtle's War in 1874, Bartholomew served as a scout for General "Mad" Anthony Wayne and was present at the 1795 signing of the Treaty of Greenville. In 1800, he moved his family into the newly created Indiana Territory and received a commission as Major in the Clark County militia on September 21, 1803. In 1806, he was promoted to lieutenant colonel. On November 7, 1811, the recently promoted full Colonel Bartholomew took part in the Battle of Tippecanoe by leading 120 militia members. During battle, Bartholomew was shot and seriously wounded in his right arm.

Later when Bartholomew's son fell ill, he volunteered to enlist as a private in his place, under the command of Colonel Russell of the 7th Regiment, to fight in the White River Campaign during the War of 1812. Colonel Russell praised Bartholomew, telling the Indiana territorial governor, "Col. Bartholomew acted as my aide-de-camp: the veteran has been so well tried in this kind of warfare, that any encomiums from me would be useless." In 1816, he was commissioned as Major General, the highest rank at that time. He served as Major General of the Indiana Militia until 1822.

After his wartime military service came to an end, Bartholomew became involved in politics. In 1818, he served on the Indiana General Assembly, and was elected to the Indiana Senate in 1820. He was selected to be a member of the commission to choose the location of the capital of Indiana, and helped pick Indianapolis as the new site. He would often claim "to have dug the first dirt for the State capital." Though he moved home in 1822, he continued to serve the state on the board of commissioners for land deeds. He retired in 1825, sold his farm and moved to McLean County, Illinois. He and his son planted a new town named Clarksville north of present-day Bloomington, Illinois, which was abandoned by the 1850s. He was an avid supporter in William Henry Harrison's presidential campaign in 1840. In the fall of that year, his health began declining and he died November 3, 1840, and is buried in Clarksville Cemetery in McLean County. His grave marker was placed by the Grand Army of the Republic in 1894 with the inscription "To the memory of Maj. Gen. Joseph Bartholomew Hero of Tippecanoe. He fought in the Revolutionary War, The War of 1812, & the Black Hawk War."

George Beck Sr.: Early Mill Owner

George Beck Sr. was born in Berks County, Pennsylvania, in 1762. As a young boy, his family moved to Rowan County, North Carolina, where he served as a private in the Continental Army of North Carolina. After moving to the Indiana Territory, Beck was at the battle of Tippecanoe, where he ranked as major. His bravery in that fight was highly commended.

On December 25, 1807, George Beck and his two sons, John and George Jr., crossed the Ohio River following the Buffalo Trace into the Indiana Territory looking for a new home. They left the rest of the family in Bear Grass, Kentucky, now known as Louisville. On their second day of travel, they left the Buffalo Trace and traveled north where they found a location to their liking and made a temporary brush shelter under a big elm tree. Later George Jr. stated that it was a common practice for many of the early settlers to make return trips to North Carolina. He said that at the age of 15, he had made that trip and walked all the way from North Carolina to Washington County, Indiana, with a gun over his shoulder.

The Beck Saw and Grist-Mill was the first in the township as well as the first in the county. This family also operated an early distillery. Beck's Mill, Indiana, was built in

1807 by George Beck Sr. Before Beck's Mill was settled, it was the site of the largest Delaware Indian village in Washington County. There was about a 15-acre clearing of trees around the spring that the Becks later used for their grain mill. A number of Indian trails in Washington County led to Beck's Mill from all directions. Today, some of the roads in the area are based on those trails because the Indians tended to take the shortest and easiest routes. People would travel for hours to get to Beck's Mill and then have to wait for two or three days to get their turn. The mill ran 24 hours a day, with George and the boys taking turns running the equipment.

Beck's Fort was built in a lot across from the mill after the September 3, 1812, Pigeon Roost Massacre which ended 17 women's and children's lives.

George Beck Sr. lived until August 16, 1847, and is buried in the Beck's Mill Cemetery.

Chapter 9
Historical Trivia of Indiana

From the seventeenth century onward the Scotch-Irish were vigorous frontiersmen, taking land where they wanted it, defending their assumed rights with rifle and texts of Bible scripture. They took with great seriousness the doctrine of fore-ordination, which they somehow translated into the notion that God had called them to take land from the Indians and soundly smite the Indians. Often lawless, they proved to be a sore affliction to the godly Quakers. But their shortcomings made them a force of incalculable importance in later history. Whatever they lacked in sweet reasonableness they made up in strength of character and vigor of mind.

The tales of the land west of the Allegheny Mountains portrayed it as a land of Eden. The virgin soil was unbelievably productive. In only three or four years, apple and peach trees would be bearing fruit. There were wide-open spaces where the Indians had burnt off the land to make it habitable for their game animals. The climate was as moderate as any of the lands the settlers had come from in Europe. The forests were full of oaks, walnuts, cypress, chestnuts and locust trees. Giant sycamore trees grew along the streams. One early traveler said that much of the landscape was "fine rich level land, with large meadows, fine clover bottoms and spacious plains covered with wild rye; the wood mainly large walnuts and hickories, here and there mixed with poplar, cherry trees and sugar trees." Like the eastern forests, there was very little under growth and tree trunks were long and straight. Early settlers found they could drive about the forests with sleds and horses. Little individual note was made of the forest trees until they became six to eight feet in diameter. In many of the six-foot diameter hardwood trees, it was 80 feet to the first limb and the trees were three feet in diameter at that height. Some large sycamore trees, which had a tendency to become hollow, were used as camping shelters by groups of hunters. The hollows were as large as a small room. There were salt lick springs so strong that they made the streams run blue. This gave the location names to Blue Licks in Kentucky and Blue River in southern Indiana.

1764 estimates of the number of braves in Indiana vary, but the high for each tribe was 300 Wea, 300 Kickapoo, 90 Mascouten, 250 Piankashaw, and 250 Miami for an estimated total of 1,200 braves. Most were living in northern Indiana under the control of Fort Ouiatanon (near West Lafayette) at the request of the French. They had tried to keep these Indians away from the influence of the British traders from the Carolinas. In the winter of 1744-45, the French had encouraged the Indians to raid and kill all the British on the Ohio and White River systems. As a result of the French policies, southern Indiana had few Indians until the Delaware Indians moved into the White River valley. The French lost control of the Indiana area with their defeat in the French and Indian War in 1763.

War Times in the Wild West

On September 4, 1779, Thomas Jefferson succeeded Patrick Henry as governor of Virginia. He had many financial problems in his new administration and ordered the Illinois Regiment back into Kentucky. The winter of 1779-1780 was particularly hard on the Midwest. Many wild and domestic animals froze to death. Food was short and the times hard. Many settlers starved or froze to death. Fortunately it was equally hard on the Indians. The old troublesome tribes in Indiana were the Wea, Chicago, Mascouten, Piankashaw, and Miami.

Spain was at war with England at this time, but not a formal ally of the colonies. The Spanish government in St. Louis authorized a mixed force of 100 or more Spaniards and a few Americans and Frenchmen to invade the northern Indiana area in January 1781. By going up the Illinois River to the Kankakee River, they took Fort St. Joseph in Michigan (near Niles). They held this lightly-defended fort, which was mainly a trading post, for 24 hours. They then retreated with booty of 24 bales of furs. While there, they prepared and signed a declaration claiming the fort and all of the surrounding territory as having been taken for the King of Spain. This short invasion became the basis for the Spanish claim to the Old Northwest Territory at the Peace Conference in Paris in 1783.

On January 3, 1782, a series of bundles were sent to the Governor of Canada from one of his Indian Agents. The accompanying letter stated the bundles contained the scalps of 43 American soldiers, 297 farmers, 88 women, 193 boys, 211 girls and 29 infants ripped from their mother's bellies. Each scalp had been tanned and marked as to when, where and how the owner had been killed—some by hatchets, some by bullets, some clubbed. The marks also showed that some had been killed defending their family, some killed in their fields farming, some had their brains bashed out, and some had been tortured and burned at the stake.

Indian warriors as well as renegade white outlaws took scalps. Some of the white raiders, while working for the British, went back to the communities where they had lived and scalped their former neighbors and relatives. The British paid a bounty for scalps. The normal pay scale was one pound for those of women and children, while the scalp of a man was worth three pounds. A live male prisoner was not worth any reward, while a teenage girl or woman prisoner was worth five pounds. Occasionally, some women brought as much as twenty pounds. The captured women were usually sold to British officers or to a trader for a life of servitude. Most written historical accounts of the women prisoners have only hinted at the treatment they received. In inquiries made to the British, they denied that their officers were buying women for their personal use. However, the British at Detroit bought women and scalps for 31 more years, until July 1813.

John Floyd wrote to John May on April 8, 1782, the following: "The savages began their hostilities in February, and are constantly ravaging the most interior parts of the country, which make it impossible for one settlement to assist another. From the number of horses already taken off by them, their design is to disable the inhabitants from removing until their intended campaign from Detroit against Fort Nelson can be carried into effect."

"One forth of the militia is called for by Genl. Clark for the purpose of fortifying the fort against a siege; but the authority of militia officers every day grows weaker and weaker, and the new invented idea of a separate state, calculated on purpose for disaffection seems to threaten us on all sides with anarchy, confusion, and destruction."

"But even suppose that the works can be completed it is impossible that Genl. Clark can defend it, a dependence on the militia is depending on a great uncertainty; especially when the enemy can float to the falls in 30 hours. It will take eight days at least before we (the militia) can be collected. ... If Genl. Clark be obliged to evacuate his post and the whole Indian army let loose among the scattered inhabitants unprepared to receive them, what must be the consequence? Is it not evident that the whole must fall a sacrifice? ... Our whole strength at this time is three hundred and seventy men, and who, according to the best calculations I can make, have eight hundred and forty helpless women and children to take care of. I omitted to mention that this number of men were exclusive of the small number remains of the Illinoise Regiment."

George Rogers Clark and His Illinoise Regiment

It was a remarkable feat to make an army out of the kind of people Clark had recruited. His training methods were rough and ready. Clark was quoted as saying, "After I had knocked down some and punished and imprisoned others, they became the best people that can be imagined." His men arrived on the battlefield in hunting shirt and breechcloth, naked of foot and limb with their bed, food and gun on their shoulders.

Montgomery and his men arrived at Kaskaskia in May 1779. These troops were fresh from the East. Life at the fort was hard. On October 10, Captain Shelby wrote Clark that it was useless to send the men out to hunt meat since there was no salt to cure it with. Shelby and thirty of his men had gone to the relief of Captain Godefroy Linctot at Ouiatanon in August and would have gone on to Fort St. Joseph except for the lack of shoes for the men.

In November 1779, George Rogers Clark wrote George Mason about his program to inform the western Indians what the American Revolution was all about. He told the Indians that the King of England oppressed people a long time ago. Englishmen moved to America, but the king sent governors and soldiers across the big water because he did not want to lose so many subjects. He wanted his laws obeyed but told the governors to treat the colonists well and take little from them until the colonies flourished. The king then informed his governors that—to quote Clark—"we had got rich and numerous enough" and it was time to pay tribute. The king sent more soldiers to make sure the colonists paid tribute, and the king intended to make the Indians pay next, said Clark. Session two of Clark's history lesson was that English taxes became so high that if "we killed a Deer they would take the skin and leave us only the meat." The English also "made us buy blankets with Corn to feed their Soldiers with." By this process, the Americans became naked. "And at last we complained—The King got mad and made his Soldiers kill some of our people and burn some of our villages. Our old men then held a great council and made the tomahawk very sharp. The young men were told to strike the English as long as they remained on the island. The braves struck and killed a great many of the English. The French King hearing of it told the Americans to be strong and if they wanted tomahawks, he would furnish them." Clark wrote to Mason: "This speech had a greater effect than I could have imagined, and did more service than a Regiment of Men could have done."

By November 1780, the Indians in Ohio had reoccupied their towns and were planning to return the visit to the homes of the Kentucky "Long Knives" in the spring of 1781. The white settlers were in a panic in 1781, and ready to depopulate the area. Clark at this time was planning the invasion of Detroit. He had gone to Virginia in the fall of 1780 and set up his plans with the governor. He thought it was a completed plan. Then it started to crumble. The British pressed an attack near Richmond, Virginia. The Pennsylvania military leader, Colonel Brodhead, did not provide the men that the government had agreed to send to Clark. The western front was having serious problems at Fort Jefferson on the Mississippi River. The war was not going well and some quiet

Tories of the Pennsylvania area decided to drink to King George's health. Other military leaders thought of Clark as a young upstart and they were jealous of his reputation and success. Some of the other colonels were interested in their own projects and glory. Their interests robbed Clark of the manpower he needed to strike a decisive blow at the Indians and British. And it got worse. The Virginia legislature passed a law fixing a "scale of depreciation" in 1781 for debts incurred. The ratio given was for the continental money vs. gold or silver coinage. In 1777, the ratio was two-and-a-half to one; in 1778, six to one; in 1779, forty to one; in 1780, seventy-five to one; and by 1781, one-thousand to one.

In a communication dated July 2, 1783, Governor Benjamin Harrison of Virginia rescinded the commission of George Rogers Clark and dismissed his services. Harrison gave the poor economic resources of Virginia as the reason. Clark was furious and bitter. The eastern military leaders thought that formal military procedure and tactics worked best in all occasions. Clark and his western troops were decidedly best at guerrilla warfare that closely matched them to their Indian foes. The Indians respected Clark for his method of fighting. Some of the east coast leaders (McIntosh, Brodhead and Washington) were not so sure of his unorthodox ways.

In the spring of 1785, the Delaware Indians sent a delegate to the Shawnee Indians in western Ohio to tell them their lands had been given to the Americans in a treaty at Fort McIntosh by tribes not living on that land. By this time, 45,000 settlers were living in Kentucky and all the better land had been claimed. The settlers wanted more land north of the Ohio River.

The Miami sponsored a grand war council at Ouiatanon in August 1785. Their purpose was to plan driving out all Americans north of the Ohio and make general war against Kentucky. The French citizens of Vincennes were terrorized in the spring of 1786 when the Wabash Indians and Americans were fighting along the Wabash. They were trying to act as arbitrators between the Indians and Americans, but were having little success. The Indians, when on the warpath, made little difference between the Americans and the English because the English had abandoned them after urging them to take up the war club during the American Revolution. Filson wrote George Rogers Clark at the request of the French and American citizens of Vincennes on March 16, 1786. They needed help before the Indians killed them all. They had scalped one settler near Vincennes and destroyed their crops and promised to return in the fall to finish their work. The people of Kentucky were reluctant to leave their homes to fight the Indians unless they were actually threatened by the tribes. Clark knew this and asked Congress for part of General Harmar's federal troops to help with this emergency. They refused, but Patrick Henry, governor of Virginia, sent instructions for 2,000 men and materials to be drafted for the cause. Clark was not happy with this arrangement because he had used drafted men before and thought it was a disaster in the making. He reluctantly took command of the 1,200 who did show up. He wanted to go directly to the Indian towns on the Wabash, but was overruled and had to wait at Vincennes for his supplies to arrive by water. The supplies were late and the beef ration had spoiled. The drafted men became mutinous on the second day of march to the Indian towns. A group of militia from Lincoln County, Kentucky, under Colonel Barrett, voted to return to Kentucky without engaging the Indians and set out for their homes when they got within one day of the villages. Clark returned to Vincennes and tried to figure out how to put the best face on his failure. He was afraid if the Indians knew what really happened they would be encouraged to do vast damage to the settlers in Indiana since they felt there was nothing to fear from the Kentucky Militia. He sent word to the Wabash tribes to come to

Clarksville for a pow wow in November; if they did not come, he would accept their absence as a desire for war. One of the French sent word that Clark had started to their villages with an army, but he had talked Clark into giving the Indians one last chance to sit and talk peace before Clark wiped them out. The chiefs were slow to reply but when they did they stated they did not want to go to Clarksville but would meet with Clark at Vincennes in April. Since this was a bluff on Clark's part, he accepted. Besides, it would help insure a relatively quiet winter for the settlers. His men were out of supplies and a fresh stock was found below Vincennes that belonged to an unlicensed Spanish trader who was suspected of trading with the Indians. Clark authorized the confiscation of the stock for the use of the army.

In June, Clark conceived the plan to separate the Shawnee Indians from their support groups of Delaware and Miami Indians by moving the other tribes farther to the north and west and away from the Shawnee. After the support tribes had been manipulated, he would then take on the main problem of the Shawnee warriors. Clark had been recommissioned a general and in October was leading an 1,800-man force deep into the Indian territory of the upper Wabash Valley with the intent to subdue the Delaware and Miami Indians. Just as the expedition was getting well underway he received intelligence that the Shawnee were mounting a large war party in Ohio. He feared an invasion of Kentucky during his absence and sent Colonel Logan back to Kentucky with instructions to form another expedition to stop that feared invasion of the Shawnee. Clark thought he was going to fight the Indians of the upper Wabash, but instead he talked peace with them. The Shawnee, who in fact were getting up a war party to assist the Delaware and Miami against Clark, got there after Clark's departure. Colonel Logan, who thought he was going to find a large Shawnee war party in Ohio, found only villages inhabited by old men, women and children. Since there were few warriors left, Logan plundered 13 Shawnee villages in the area and destroyed their winter food stocks.

Without Clark, Wisconsin, Michigan, Ohio, Indiana, and Illinois would probably be part of Canada today. Some of the citizens of the west were desirous of complete separation of this area from the original 13 colonies. Many turned on Clark for his loyalty to the colonies. James Wilkinson's intrigues to destroy Clark's reputation and the government's lack of support for the efforts of Clark came back to haunt the government. Other professional military leaders tried to organize armies to defeat the troublesome Indians after the government relieved Clark of command in the Old Northwest Territory. Their efforts were utter and dismal failures. In 1791, when Indian problems were again starting to be a headache, Thomas Jefferson wrote to a Western friend to see if he could encourage Clark to again lead the army. By now George was a sadder but wiser man.

There was a hollow echo in the mind of Clark of the words of Thomas Jefferson, Wythe and Mason; the final sentence of the letter of January 3, 1778, was "WE THINK YOU MAY SAFELY CONFIDE IN THE JUSTICE AND GENEROSITY OF THE VIRGINIA ASSEMBLY."

Throughout the war, Clark and his men received no pay for their services. Furthermore, Clark was held responsible for debts incurred for supplies since Virginia, despite its promises, never reimbursed him. Clark was appointed an Indian Commissioner after the war, and in 1786 he helped negotiate a treaty with the Shawnees. The same year, he led an expedition against the Wabash tribes and seized goods taken to Vincennes by Spanish traders.

James Wilkinson, a double agent in the pay of Spain, coveted Clark's command and his post of Indian commissioner. After a deliberate campaign to discredit Clark, Wilkinson was appointed Indian commissioner and Clark was relieved of his military command.

On February 7, 1784, 27-year-old General James Wilkinson sent a written message to the Indian chiefs asking them to come and talk peace, and told them the military troops were to be dismissed in the west since there was no need for them. Major Walls dismissed the Regulars of the Illinois Regiment at Louisville on February 15th. The government cut down the army to 100 men. Major Walls did stay in his Louisville office in case the Indians wanted to come and talk of peace. The results in the west were what everyone but a Congressman could perceive—more Indian troubles with no standing army to hold them in check. The "Virginia Calendar" later recorded the names of more than 1,500 men, women and children killed and scalped in Kentucky between 1783 and 1790. It also estimated that between 2,000 and 20,000 horses were stolen in the same period of time. In 1786, an Indian shot and killed the grandfather of Abraham Lincoln 18 miles east of Louisville. The Indian was killed by one of Lincoln's sons before the Indian could scalp "old Abraham."

Clark was a follower of Jefferson, but Jefferson's republican principles were taking the American Experiment in a direction the aristocracy and their federalist principles could not stand. Jefferson thought the Federalist Party had designs to implant monarchist ideals and institutions in the government. He thought the people were to be trusted and given control of their own destiny, and labored to check the authoritarian control of the government. The marks of his administration were the reduction of internal taxes, the military budget cut, and the planning to do away with the public debt. The right of the oldest heir to inherit all of the family property was also to be discouraged. Jefferson held three causes dear to his heart. They were freedom from Britain, freedom of conscience and freedom maintained through education. The aristocracy blocked Jefferson, and those who supported him, whenever it could because his plans were directly at odds with their plans and dreams for America.

To quote Peter S. Onuf, a 20th century Thomas Jefferson historian, "The Federalists had no intention of winning the war in the West, the rapid distribution of public lands would have cleared the Ohio country of Indians without any assistance from a 'military establishment.' But it was in the Federalists interest to keep the frontiers aflame."

John Taylor, a critic of the Federalists in 1790, wrote, "An expensive and unsuccessful war, may cultivate the public mind into a willingness to treat away this territory to the Indians." As a result, the conditions of Virginia's 1784 land cession, the model for subsequent state cessions, would not be fulfilled. Public lands would not be sold at reasonable prices to industrious settlers, thus helping discharge the nation's revolutionary debts, nor would frontier settlements be formed into new states "in faithful compliance with the solemn compacts long since entered into with the ceding states." Scarcely a financial boon, the national domain would instead be a constant drain on the Treasury and a justification for higher taxes. "Nothing is wanting to consummate the system," Taylor concluded, "but a relinquishment of the right of preemption to the Indians, beyond the Ohio. So that the Indians and British may mount guard over the growth of republicanism in that quarter." This lack of support by the federalists in the central government may explain why only token support was given to Clark when a few thousand men would have decisively changed the western frontier; and why Clark died a bitter, alcoholic old man. It would also explain why the trumped-up charges leveled on Clark by Wilkinson were so eagerly believed by the east coast elite in government and used as an excuse to withdraw support from Clark.

After the Revolutionary War

On September 11, 1783, 360 Indians and 40 Queen's Rangers under Captain John Pratt set out to siege Wheeling, Virginia. They anticipated a victory as great as Blue Licks. Wheeling was defended by only 63 souls—30 men, 17 wives, 12 unmarried girls and four boys—and an ancient French swivel cannon. With pluck, luck and a few well placed cannon shots, Fort Henry defended itself with great valor from the Indians and British. Some historians state that the last shots fired by British soldiers in the Revolutionary War were fired in this battle. The British and Indians withdrew on September 13th. The Revolution was over. Clark was broke. Those who gave Clark credit were broke. The Virginia government was broke and not interested in paying claims on land that they had ceded to the federal government. Worst yet, the land claims of most of the war leaders were found to be faulty as the eastern land sharks and legal mosquitoes moved west. The Indians could be handled because they were honorable, but not this new breed of scalper. The western settlers were largely illiterate and could not fight this war of words. What to do?

The answer was two fold. One was to survey the land by range and township descriptions and not allow the meet and bounds type of description to continue in land transactions. It was the meet and bounds descriptions that had caused so much trouble for the early settlers in Kentucky. The second was to move to new frontiers, but which ones? The land to the far north was occupied by people who were plotting to burn out the western colonists. They were not welcome there. Michigan and Wisconsin areas were yet to open. Indiana and Illinois lands were tempting. Many pioneer settlers went west to Missouri and parts of the lower Mississippi Valley. Some went to Central America. Spanish Louisiana was a magnet. Daniel Boone moved to the St. Charles, Missouri, area. Some settled at the mouth of the Yazoo River in what is now Mississippi. A one-hundred-mile-square area west of the Ohio and Mississippi junction in Missouri was offered for settlement. In 1786, the soldiers and their families were on the move again, this time for homesteads to hunt and farm, not forts to defend.

Jefferson, who understood this restless people very well, did much to encourage further western expansion. He asked George Rogers Clark to head up an expedition to find a passage to the Pacific. George turned down the offer. His youngest brother, William, accepted. With the authorization of the Lewis and Clark Expedition and the Pike Expeditions between 1804 and 1807, the road map for further expansion was set. Jefferson's belief seems to have been that if you cannot settle the people down, then keep them moving west to the benefit of all.

In May 1786, orders were given by Governor Patrick Henry to build a fort at the falls and detach two companies of federal troops to man it. Major Finney built Fort Finney II on the north side of the Ohio River at the top of the chute going into the falls. This site is now in the Ohio River at the end of Fort Street near Front Street in Jeffersonville, Indiana, directly below Interstate 65 under the Kennedy Bridge. This fort was built on top of the high ground since a spring flood had destroyed Fort Finney I at the mouth of the Great Miami River in Ohio. Fort Finney II was later renamed Fort Steuben. However, the entire Ohio River valley had a great flood in 1793, and the few settlers who had their cabins in the rich lowlands were forced to retreat to higher ground for safety, while their fences and, in some cases, their cabins floated away. Fort Stueben must have been salvageable since the Indiana Militia used it into the 1820's. At a later date, even the ground upon which the fort was built was swept away by the turbulent floods of the Ohio River.

The east coast upper class had a true fear of the western illiterates. What the east coast elite had done to England, with their withdrawal from British control, they were afraid their western brothers would do to them. The nation was in deep debt. The logistics of developing this vast new area concerned them. They were afraid the citizens of the west would cause more debt and expect to vote their eastern brothers to pay the bills. At the Philadelphia Convention in 1787, Elbridge Gerry of Massachusetts suggested that the number of representatives chosen from the west should NEVER exceed the number chosen by the Atlantic states. Now, only the national government could issue money, the states had lost that right, and the west was desperately short of paper money.

The Spanish controlled the West's door to the world—New Orleans. They were threatening to close that door. Through Colonel Wilkinson's influence, the Spanish wanted the upper Mississippi and Ohio River watershed to recede from the United States and become part of the Spanish empire. In 1785, John Jay proposed giving up American rights to navigate the Mississippi for twenty-five years in exchange for a favorable trade treaty with Spain. The new government on the east coast was trying to stack itself against the uneducated and irresponsible citizens of the West. None of these prospects sat well with western settlers.

Alexander Hamilton, a Federalist, proposed to raise federal income by a method that would not offend his friends in the eastern commercial group. He proposed a tax on whiskey production. This hit hard at the small farmers of the backcountry. The sale of whiskey by this group was about the only way they had to raise a little cash. Now the government wanted a part of that profit. Washington backed Hamilton with federal troops to crush the "Whiskey Rebellion." The resentment in the West was great. This tax was the start of the Internal Revenue Service in the United States.

The proud but uneducated people of the Ohio Valley had three exterior problems that irritated them like a bee sting. The Indians were harassing their lives with support of traders who wanted to protect their source of fur-bearing animals in the Northwest Territory. The Spanish threatened their economic lives by closing the port of New Orleans; and the Federalist government kept making rules that they did not think reasonable. In their minds the answer was simple: (1) go to Canada and get rid of the British who sponsored the actions of the Indians; (2) float down the river to New Orleans and "clean out" the problematic Spanish administration; and (3) elect men to take over the government from the Federalists, or start their own government.

On March 1, 1784, Virginia gave up her western lands to the United States of America. The federal government proposed to make 10 states out of this region. Their names were to be Sylvania, Chersonesus, Michigania, Washington, Saratoga, Metropotamia, Assenipia, Illinoia, Polypotamia and Pelisipia. Two of the states were to be north of the Ohio River to the 39th parallel. Their common border was to be a meridian drawn through the falls of the Ohio River. East of that meridian was to be Polypotamia. West of that meridian was to be Pelisipia.

Troubles in the Indiana Territory

Governor William Henry Harrison was a young officer under "Mad" Anthony Wayne in his campaign at Fallen Timbers, Ohio, and used his experiences with Wayne to guide him later in his rise to power. The Indians were peaceful for several years. William Henry was a son of Virginia governor Benjamin V. Harrison.

The census of 1800 indicated there were only 5,641 residents in the Indiana Territory. Kentucky had 220,955. The economic hard times following the Revolutionary War sent many settlers into Kentucky, Tennessee and the Old Northwest Territory along the Ohio River. Slavery had been an issue in the Indiana Territory. In 1802, a convention at Vincennes petitioned Congress to allow slavery in the Territory. Congress turned down the petition. The next year, a Virginia law that permitted servants to bind themselves to their master for a stated period of time, including life, was adopted. When this law was repealed in 1810 there were 250 slaves in the total Indiana population of 25,000. While Indiana was the most southern of the northern states, in the Northwest Territory slavery was not popular because the economic reality was that a sturdy yeoman could not compete with unpaid slave labor.

Aaron Burr, Jefferson's vice president, was asked by his political rivals to be their candidate for governor of New York. The Federalist plan was to elect Burr governor and then take New York and New England out of the Union. Hamilton learned of the plot and exposed it. With its failure Burr was completely discredited and to satisfy his honor he challenged Hamilton to a duel. Burr killed Hamilton in 1804.

In 1806, Aaron Burr went west to restart his political career and found support with people who did not trust the government. His plan was to assemble 1,000 men in Ohio, float down the river and take New Orleans with the help of a British fleet. He would then form a new independent state in Louisiana under British control with Burr as head of state. Burr had considerable support from people who were later the early settlers of southern Indiana. In the winter of 1806-1807, Burr's forces were stationed at Jeffersonville. Wilkinson betrayed the plot to the government and Burr was tried for treason.

Some of Burr's followers fled into the frontier lands of southern Indiana for personal safety from possible prosecution. John Gibson wrote in a letter to Captain William Hargrove, the head of the Rangers, on August 13, 1807. In it he stated, "The camp that your scout Fuquay found east of the trace to Yellow Bank are no doubt a part of the misguided people who have scattered over the country as fugitives from justice, that had assembled at an island up the Ohio river as followers of that arch traitor and murderer, Aaron Burr. The governor has closely interrogated Fuquay and this is his opinion, the people are guilty of no more wrong than that of being duped by one of the smartest villains in the country. They only acted as was dictated to them by those who held and had held high positions in the Government. It is broadly hinted that a man high in military command in the American army (Wilkinson) was strongly tinctured with Burr's chimerical conspiracy that saved him from disgrace by turning a traitor to Burr. The thing to do is for you to have these four misguided men with their wives and helpless children, prepare a fort some place where you think best in your military territory so that you can give them your protection. Your good judgment is depended upon to keep this matter close and so instruct the refugees. Fuquay has been obligated to secrecy. These people are no doubt worthy and will grow up among the other pioneers and be useful to our country. You will find out from them if they know of any other bands in hiding. This territory needs more people and these misguided, duped men and women will make as good citizens as any."

A week later Gibson again wrote Hargrove. "Your report by the Crea Indian. He was detained here to carry you this letter of instruction. The four young men you sent with him have enlisted and look like good material to make soldiers. The Governor is well pleased with your success in having the four families located in your district. The young men you sent were interrogated separately. They all agree in their statements that there are several other bands scattered over your territory some distance north of the Ohio river from ten to fifteen miles east of yellow bank trace to something like the same distance west of the same trace. They claim that there is one band of these refugees west of the Yellow Bank trace about ten miles. They were camped near a large creek. It is thought best for you to send FuQuay, with two other men, to find these people and have them locate in a place that they can be given protection and they can aid in giving protection to others. Young Bailey, one of the men you sent in some time ago has orders to report to you to go with FuQuay. He is acquainted with the people and has been in their camp. He says that there are six men, three women and five children in the band. Instruct FuQuay to inform the refugees that they must move near some of the settled sections and build a block house for their protection and there will be no questions asked."

Governor William Henry Harrison advised Captain Hargrove in a letter of October 4, 1807, the following: "The two men coming into your lines east of the Mud-hole have certainly repented of all the wrong which they have done by following after Traitor Burr. It is best for you to see all these people who are connected with that unfortunate affair and instruct them under no circumstances to let any one know that they were in the Burr conspiracy. If they do in after years they will be accused of being traitors by people not half so worthy as they are."

Occasionally the Rangers would discover other troublesome individuals who were not what they appeared to be while they were on patrol. John Gibson's letter of October 12, 1807, to Hargrove hints at a portion of that problem. Gibson stated, "Your report, and the man you sent in under guard, are here. You did the right thing in arresting this man, all suspicious cases, as this should be investigated. What this man is has not been found out and it is doubtful if it ever is. If this country were at war with a white race it would evidently be determined that he was a spy locating the military strength and positions of our army. It may be that he is doing that work for the British. He evidently is not what he claims to be. A prisoner for two years among the Indians would not have such clean underwear beneath his buckskin suit. Then a barber has recently cut his hair. He will be detained for the present."

While the settlers and the Indians were at nominal peace in southern Indiana Territory, there were some raids, and settlers killed and scalped by the Indians. Governor William Henry Harrison organized a group of men into the Indiana Rangers in 1807. Their duties were to patrol the southern part of Indiana and respond to and pursue any atrocity to a settler by the Indians. The rangers were divided into three divisions. The first division patrolled from the Wabash to French Lick. The second patrolled from French Lick to the Falls of the Ohio. The third patrolled from the Falls of the Ohio to the Ohio state line. Their patrolling was effective and the number of Indian raids decreased to nearly nothing.

Harrison disbanded them in 1809 because he thought they had accomplished what they had set out to do. He called them back as the War of 1812 started. A total of 4,160 volunteers were raised for the border defense. They were loosely organized into six militia regiments. Only sixteen companies were actually called into active service.

Harrison appointed a commission to organize Harrison County in 1808, and the county was formed on October 11, 1808. Corydon was laid out the same year and the first court was held there on May 10, 1809. Towns older than Corydon in this area were Marvin, across from Brandenburg, Kentucky, and Northampton, six miles down the Ohio from Marvin. The frontier of the state in 1810 was along the east fork of White River from Fort Vallonia (established 1807) to Bono, and Hindostan Falls.

The 1809 Treaty of Fort Wayne by Harrison opened parts of southern Indiana for settlement. The land acquisitions of Harrison and the pressures put on by the white settlers contributed to Indiana's participation in the War of 1812. Most of the Indians sided with the British and moved to the northern part of the territory, close to their protectors. This helped open up more of southern Indiana for land concessions by the Indians. However, with the start of the Indian Raids in 1811, the exposed area near Fort

Vallonia saw a decrease of settler families. Where there had been 70 families, after the raids started about 50 families moved back to more secure settlements. Some went as far as Kentucky for safety.

The charter of the Bank of the United States expired in 1811. For money the country had to rely on individual and corporation notes, foreign coins, cut money, and a few United States coins then in circulation. More manufactured products were coming into the western territory than there was money to pay for them. There was a severe shortage of cash in this area, but an abundance of resources yet to be tapped. Kentucky was in a period of wild speculation. Inflation and speculation were rampant. Getting into debt was one alternative to ruin. The bubble burst and one of the ways out led across the river into Indiana.

The unglaciated area north of the Ohio River was a magnet to the settlers. This thin-soiled Knobstone Escarpment, with rugged hills rising four to six hundred feet above the valleys, does not seem highly desirable by today's standards. To the early settler it appeared to be the best of lands. It was well-drained and had an abundance of springs and forest decay for humus. The woods supplied game and forage for the stock. In the small valleys, acreage was large enough for hand cultivation. The higher levels were free from mosquitoes and the ague (malaria). Sickness was not as prevalent as in the bottomlands. Travel on horseback was easier than in the low marshy flood plains of the river valleys.

The citizens of this period were daring and hardy hunters, content with the rudest shelters, a corn and pumpkin patch, and a few hogs of the same bold disposition as themselves. Some times they had a cow. Expert with a rifle, vindictive against the Indians, often mild mannered, withal honest, inclined to move often and heeding little to the trappings of land titles or the refinements of civilization, these men of the "long knife" stock were not tenderfeet, for back of them was usually more than one generation of pioneers. The first settlers were hardly distinguishable from the hunter. They were half-hunter, half-farmer. They possessed more of the utensils of civilization than the hunter but were willing to sell out and move on at the slightest encouragement. They were, in short, "HOOSIERS."

To the foreign traveler, Indiana seemed a decided change for the worse. Kentucky politeness and hospitality gave way to impudence, ignorance, and laziness. The Hoosier dialect, the nasal twang, the provincial expressions became more noticeable in the speech. One traveler said, "We are now quite out of society; everything, everybody, with some few exceptions, looks wild and half savage." Hoosiers were thought to be lawless, semi-barbarous vagabonds, dangerous to live among.

The War of 1812 on the western front was the culmination of 50 years of sporadic guerrilla warfare with the Indians. A newspaper of the times summed up the feelings as follows: "We have had but one opinion as to the cause of the depredations of the Indians. They are instigated and supported by the British in Canada." The slogan of many War Hawks on the frontier was "ON TO CANADA."

Harrison knew the true value of the local untrained militia, men whom he once described as being as dependable in battle as a mob "bearing sticks." Individually they were fearless, good trackers, and marksmen with a knack for living off the land, but they had little respect for organization or authority. Most of the men owned and were experts in using a flintlock rifle known as the "Kentucky Rifle." Its unique features made it the superior weapon of its day. Its range was three times as far as the smoothbore that it replaced. Its accuracy was better and it used less powder. The men were motivated by the realization of many generations of dreams in their family. They owned land and were the proud "Lord of the Manor" equal to any and servant to none. They truly believed they were in the land of the free and home of the brave. To keep that dream, they had only to defend that homestead. Harrison avoided using them, except for defensive purposes, until his few regular officers could instruct them in the rudiments of soldiering.

John Tipton kept a daily journal of the campaign to Tippecanoe. It gave a day-to-day insight into military life far different from what we would expect of a crack military unit set with a single-minded determination to slay the enemy. The first part of the journal states that both Spencer's 47-man unit and Heth's 22-man unit traveled together. Other southern Indiana units joined them as they marched to Vincennes. A lot of the time was spent looking for lost horses, hunting and finding bee trees, hunting game, having shooting matches and getting drunk. He mentioned "mutinized with some of Capt. Heaths men but marched back at Sun set and Dismisst in order." The next day "my self and three others got parted from the company and lay al night by our selves only with too of Capt. Heths men." "When they got to Vincennes, Capt. Spencer and a tavern keeper treated the men to drink. Much whiskey was drunk which caused quarreling amont the men." Among the many bee trees that the unit found, Tipton recounted that from one they harvested nine or 10 gallons of honey. When the unit was in the field for about three weeks, Tipton said that Captain Heath was sick and his men dismissed for the day. The men were becoming restless and wanted to go home. To keep from being too bored, they had wrestling matches, "pulled corn" from Indian corn fields, and had sham fights in the woods. About the time that General Harrison told the men that they would have to fight the Indians, a few men started to desert and strike out for home. Tipton mentioned that the captain and the sergeant had quarreled on Sunday, October 20th, and the next day the company's 2nd lieutenant resigned and went home.

On October 24th, a man was drummed out of camp with his head shaved and powdered. While Tipton was watching this, someone burnt Captain Spencer's tent. Later, Captain Spencer and 10 men left camp to scout the area without authorization. General Harrison threatened to break the officers involved when they got back. Spencer got back very late that night and was very sick the next day. Several times Tipton mentioned drawing his whiskey ration. One time when he was out for four days, he got a gallon when he got back. At another time he mentioned that he "had one quort of whisky yesterday and one today."

On November 6th, Tipton wrote, "found we ware near the Celebrated Prophet,s town. Stopt in a Prairie. The Foot throwd all their napsacks in the waggons we formd in order of Battle marchd 2 miles then formd the line of Battle we marchd in 5 lines on the extreme Right went in to a Cornfield then up to the above town and Surrounded it they met us Pled for Peace they said they would give us Satisfac[tion] in the morning... agreeable to their Promise Last night we ware answered by the firring of guns and the Shawnies Brakeng into our tents a blood Combat took place at precisely 15 minuts Before five in the morning which Lasted 2 hours and 20 minuts."

The famous battle had come and gone. Tecumseh was not yet there with the 2,000 southern Indians, but he was on the way. His late arrival probably saved the lives of the remaining American soldiers. He had warned his brother, the Prophet, not to attack the American army until his return and wait for the "Greats Sign."

The great New Madrid earthquake occurred on December 16, 1811, and was followed by two more on January 23 and February 13, 1812. George Beck stated that the aftershocks could be felt for over forty days. Some of them were strong enough that people were shaken in their beds. Suspended items in the barns would swing as much as six inches. The joints of the cabins creaked, and some were moved out of place. Many chimneys were knocked down. The shocks were quick and violent. Five or six times the ground waved like a field of tall grass in the wind. Logs loaded on wagons were known to fall to the ground. The shocks were felt as far east as Pittsburgh.

The Indians took the earthquakes as the spiritual signs Tecumseh had called for to signal the Indians to unite and throw out the settlers. The British in Canada were outfitting the Indians with new guns. Hostilities across most of the frontier began in earnest. Even though the battles would be hot and heavy, the die had been cast as to the outcome. Harrison had caused the Prophet to violate his direct orders from Tecumseh by starting the battle before the Indians were ready. The settlers would ultimately be victorious.

In a letter dated July 29, 1812, from John Gibson to Colonel Hargrove, Gibson warned Hargrove to be on the lookout for a British spy who had been at Vincennes and claimed to be a expert engineer experienced in building forts. He had letters of recommendation that were very impressive, so he was given a free run of the fort to inspect it and the barracks. On the 28th the man disappeared, taking a good horse belonging to Colonel Decker, as well as a fine saddle and a brace of pistols. Gibson went on to say, "I will remind here again inform you that in the near future there is danger ahead if the war lasts any length of time. This lull is only the forerunner of certain stirring times. Be sure that everything is in readiness for what may come." Two weeks later, Gibson again wrote, "Two scouts from this post...saw two old Delaware Indian men who...were friendly and have been for a long time. They said several Pottawattamies had recently been at that point and told them, 'Soon we will go to the Ohio river—get heap horses—maybe get scalps—the British drive Americans away soon.' The scouts report that there is a general movement among the Indians, a sort of nervous unrest that forebodes trouble and that the Indians did not seem to show that hearty friendship as formerly."

Lieutenant Colonel John B. Campbell was charged with organizing an American strike force against the Indians on the Mississinewa River. He organized 787 officers and enlisted men for that task. They left Franklintown, Ohio, on November 15, 1812. They struck at the Munsee Delaware village on December 17. The men were away on a hunt and primarily only women and children were present. The tragedy was that the Indians were considered to be friendly Indians.

Early History of Jackson County recalls the adventures of David Sturgeon. While in the service of Captain Bigger's Rangers, Sturgeon recalls the massacre of a father and son near the Washington-Orange county line and the tracking and apprehension of the offending Indians. Three dead Indians and the scalped settler were found at a cabin. Bigger's men killed two more Indians when they rushed them from ambush near the cabin. The rest of the Indians retreated and were trailed to the river's edge where another was shot as he crossed the river. He sank below the water and did not resurface. One of the Rangers was shot and died that night of his wounds.

In another incident, Sturgeon recalled finding two burned cabins where seven scalped bodies lay in the still smoking ruins. Again they followed the Indians and overtook about a dozen of them attacking another cabin. As the Indians fled, they left one dead and one mortally wounded comrade. The wounded Indian looked at them defiantly. They held him prisoner in the cabin, and though in great pain, he said not a word and died without a moan, without a sigh. To the early settlers, the Indians' resolve was not an idle threat.

Some other Indian fighters operating in this area were John Beck, Micajah Callaway, John Zink, Tart Fordyce and Henry Dawalt. John Zink was mortally wounded near Columbus while chasing Indians. He died near Vallonia and was buried near Salem.

Colonel Robert M. Evans, who at one time was in charge of the militia, while making inspection of the forces somewhere in the woods where Jackson County now is (possibly on Tipton Creek near the community of Houston), with his cavalry escort, came up to the place where Major Tipton was giving some directions to mounted spies — Tipton, not paying the Colonel what Evans thought was proper military attention. Evans said, "What is your name, sir?" Tipton turned around in his saddle and looking at him said, "If that is of any importance, Colonel, my name is John Tipton." "Where are your headquarters?" asked the Colonel. The Major replied, "Is now on this saddle, and tonight, sir, if I can find a tree without a panther being at roost in it, it will be on this saddle at the root of that tree." The Colonel, being a very dignified man and much used to formality, in making his report to Governor Gibson, said; "That varmint that you have on duty up in the wilds of Harrison County paid no more attention to me than he would have to an ordinary man."

In 1813, the Indians did not attack forts or blockhouses, but small Indian scouting parties often penetrated the settlements, eluded the vigilance of the rangers, killed one or more settlers, stole horses and escaped from the hot pursuit of the militia. On the 18th of February, a man was killed about twenty miles below Vincennes. On the third of March, two white men were killed and twenty horses stolen seven miles west of Vincennes. On the 13th of March, two men were killed near Brookville and three killed in Wayne County. On March 16, the Indians raided the Leesville settlement—two men were killed and one wounded. The McMurtry family was traveling into the new territory. Indians ambushed them near Salem, Indiana. The parents were killed and scalped; the two children were led off. The son was never heard of again; the daughter was rescued in October of 1813, by some of her Kentucky neighbors after the Battle of the Thames in Canada, where the Indians had sold her into slavery to a British officer. Since the British claimed that no female captives were ever sold to British officers, the American military officers took a sworn statement from her to the fact that she had been sold into slavery to a British officer

A small boat was attacked near Fort Harrison with two killed and six wounded on March 28. On April 16, two were killed (the Solidad brothers) and one wounded about eight miles southwest of Vallonia.

In May 1813, the Indiana Militia was increased by twelve companies. The purpose of the increase was to station more companies in exposed parts of the territory. In June 1813, three or four companies of rangers and militia made a sudden raid on several Indian villages of the west fork of White River and reduced them to ashes, together with a considerable quantity of corn and other supplies. The braves who had been harassing the border had their headquarters there. The rangers were determined to root them out. The braves were gone but the plan was successful. Another militia group under Lieutenant Colonel John Tipton left Vallonia on June 11 to pursue a course north and northeast about 100 miles to the upper Delaware towns on the White River, but most of the villages had already been burnt a few weeks earlier.

In July 1813, Colonel William Russell was preparing an expedition at Vallonia against the Indians and marched through central Indiana with a strong mounted corps of rangers and volunteer militia. The combined forces of this group were 500 strong, including 100 from Kentucky. Colonel Russell found no Indians on his 400-mile march. It was surmised that Tecumseh and 1,000 Indians had left in late April and had gone to Malden, Canada, to assist General Proctor in his campaign against General Harrison.

The frontier was a fluid and moving entity. In 1795, the frontier was at the Ohio River. By 1812, the frontier had moved to the east fork of White River. By 1818, it had moved farther north to the west fork of White River. By 1822, it had moved to the upper Wabash and Tippecanoe River. By 1830, it had moved out of Indiana. The wildest of days had come and gone. Now the citizen had to put up with the mundane progress of "civilization." The crusty individual who had made it possible to claim the title of the territory from the British and wrestle dominance of the land from the Indian was now becoming out of place. The gears of society were slowly shifting.

Life in Early Indiana

L and was the chief source of wealth in a world that had little money. The lack of good land at a reasonable price in the east motivated most of the land-hungry settlers west.

Land gave its owner security and social status. While pioneer life was hard in the Indiana Territory, many people thought of it as the happiest time in their life. Coarse food and rough diet were the order of the day, but every cabin was a relief of want. There was no heaped up wealth, all were equal in the outback. When they gathered, there was levity, jollity, frankness and liberal affection for each other. They did not try to put each other down At the end of the War of 1812, land in Indiana was worth $1.25 to $5.00 an acre. As close as Cincinnati, Ohio, unimproved land was worth $30.00 an acre. It was hoped that the Indiana land would soon be worth as much. The land office was using easy credit policy for the purchase of this land. Speculation was wild in land purchase. The boom was on.

In the Indiana Territory, wild game was easy to find. Bear, deer, wild turkeys, pigeons, opossums, ducks, geese, partridges, quail, prairie chicken, parakeets, squirrels and lesser game were so common that they were a nuisance. At times, wild turkey were so tame that they had to be kept away from the corn when the hogs were fed, and if one was wanted, a fat specimen was selected and hit in the head with a club. Deer were known to eat the entire tobacco crop of the settlers. Fish were so common in White River that half-acre schools of them were observed just below the surface. Early fishermen did not brag on how many fish they caught, but on how many BARRELS of fish they caught. Some of the choicest treats of the frontier were wildcat and rattlesnake meat, which was found as "sweet and white as an eel." Hunting was the pleasure sport of the day. At this time, it was the potato, pumpkin and grain crops that were in short supply. Salt and flour were treats in the frontier home.

There was a limited number of buffalo in the southern part of Indiana when the first white settlers came into this area around 1810. They were not known to migrate as readily as their western cousins. They had the habit of staying in smaller herds along the river and creek bottoms. They grazed on the grasses and rich growth of cane in the foothills around the bottoms. The herds had a keen sense of smell and could scent danger at a great distance. It was difficult for the early settlers to get close enough to shoot them. However, if they could be killed, the settlers found their flesh as good or better than the best stall-fed beef. It had a slight wild, venison taste that gave it an excellent flavor savored by the early settler. The usual weight of a grown buffalo was around a thousand pounds. A few of the buffalo were domesticated and were valuable at drawing heavy loads.

The limited number of buffalo found here by the first settlers is thought to be because the panthers were the predator kings of the dense woods of southern Indiana. The panthers were known to perch in trees near the salt licks and pounce upon their prey as they went under their lairs. Their two-inch claws would be embedded into the flesh of their prey and it was nearly impossible for the large forest animals to tear loose or throw the panther off their backs. This was true for the buffalo, elk and occasional Indian. The panthers would not attack a human if they were face to face. They would usually turn their eyes from side to side and try to avoid a direct stare and nervously pat their tail on the ground. But the moment the man turned, they would pounce on their prey. Their habit was to eat their fill of their kill and bury the remains for a later meal. They would cover the carcass with grass, leaves and brush, then rest nearby to watch their cache.

Another predator of the woods of southern Indiana was the timber wolf. The wolves were about the size of a large dog and traveled in packs. Their hunting tactics were usually to surround their large prey and harass it from all directions until the animal was exhausted, and then they would charge the exhausted animal for the kill. Smaller animals were just run down, overpowered and killed. The individual wolf's temperament was surly and cowardly. The early settlers had a hard time raising sheep because the wolves would form large packs in the woods near the sheep pens and slaughter the sheep if they were left out in the open, or howl for hours at a time if the sheep were securely penned for the night. The mounting livestock losses caused the early government to put a bounty on wolves ears.

The elk was another animal of our southern Indiana forests. The first settlers from Kentucky described the Indiana elks as larger than those found in Kentucky. The body of the elk was shaped much like a deer's, but many times larger. The elk were shy animals that were easily spooked. When disturbed, they were known to run three or four miles before stopping. The animals were hunted for their skin, which was useful to the first settlers for many purposes. Their meat was dark and coarse but very nutritious.

The black bear was a common neighbor of the first settlers until 1820. Normally the bear was timid and possessed a degree of curiosity. While his normal diet was herbs and berries, he would eat anything he could scavenge. He particularly liked the pigs of the settlers. This cost many a bear and its cubs their lives. One of the favorite sports of the early communities in southern Indiana was the bear hunt. While the bear was normally a quiet resident of the woods, it became a fearsome 450-pound fighting dynamo, as many a crippled hunting dog could attest. Besides the good sport of a bear hunt, the meat and fat were highly prized by the whites. The ham and bacon were thought to be as good as that of a pig and many of the medical remedies of this early time used bear fat to carry the herbs in the poultices used by pioneers.

By 1819, the U.S. Government was troubled with too much credit on the books and no cash to service that debt. It stopped accepting payment on its credit in local bank notes or state-backed banks. The European market for the food produce of the west had collapsed after the European wars ended. Now England was dumping manufactured products on America at below-cost prices. What little money America had was being drawn off to Europe to pay for the cheap goods. A panic and bust followed. Grumbling in the West was great. The villains were "those East coast bankers and politicians." The discontent led to some wanting to get out of the union and take their debt-ridden land with them. Fortunately, there was more land to the west and it was easier to move than fight the system. Congress did pass some relief laws for easing the repayment of the land contracts. In 1820, Congress passed legislation lowering land prices to $1.25 an acre and dropping the allotment size to 80 acres. Optimism returned to the frontier as land speculation resumed.

The early settlers had little property and no sentiment to tie them to the soil. They had log cabins, rude furniture, a drove of hogs, a herd of cows, a scrawny pony and a passle of chickens. To move was a simple matter, for all they had to do was call up the hogs and cows, pack the pony, line up the "old lady" and kids, box up the chickens, call the dog, spit on the fire and strike out. This pattern of movement was keyed to the culture of the frontier society. The first move occurred in the settlers' early twenties, when young men left their parents and got married. A decade later, as the arrival of young children put pressure on small holdings, they moved again. Ten or twenty years later, men and women in their forties and fifties looked to move once more, to find a place sufficiently open that their grown children could settle close to their elders and be a comfort to them in their later years.

Some of the eastern newspapers described the life west of the Appalachian Mountains as follows: "All is ease, tranquility, and comfort. Every person, no matter how poor, may with moderate industry, become in a very short time a landholder; his substance increases from year to year, his barns are filled with abundant harvests; his cattle multiply, his children active, vigorous and enterprising...a paradise of pleasure is opened in the wild."

Despite all the hardships of frontier life, the frontier man was essentially an optimist. Earlier, the Federalist leaders in New England were afraid their western cousins would take their money to help capitalize this new land, now they were afraid that all their neighbors would move to this land of opportunity. One traveler, Gershom Flagg, wrote back East, saying of the West, "There is no regulation for education the young in common schools. The inhabitants are from all parts north and east of Kentucky and are the most ignorant people I ever saw."

The speech of these settlers was Anglo-Saxon and Elizabethan English with influences of Pennsylvania Dutch and Indian. Their talk included such words as "blowed," "ketched," "drawed," "knowed," "seed," and "skun." They "heered" or "hearn say." Such expressions as "me and her was a sparking," "she seed he and I a-comin down the road," and "hit shore is me" were common. Adjectives were formed to suit the occasion, such as "hindleggy," "sheepsy," "sweet-meaty," "mud-piest," "dry-uppedest," "shut-pocketdest," "up and comin'dest," "fritter-minded," "lickety-brindle," and "lolly-gaggin."

Other pioneer expressions were "bound" (determined), "cazan" (cause), "fitten" (decent), "heap" (a great deal), "passel" (a parcel of people, etc.), "red up" (tidy up), "middlin" (fair, tolerable), "techous" (touchy), "piddlin" (trifling), "douncy" (half sick), "crick" (creek), "cumfluttered" (confused), and "beatenest" (hard to beat). Some of the expressions are still occasionally heard in southern Indiana. From the Indians we got such words as pecan, hickory, paw paw, raccoon, persimmon, squash, pone, canoe, moccasin, skunk, and chipmunk.

American Liberty and Freedom

"Liberty" and "freedom" are strange words. They mean similar but different things to various people. All feel comfortable with their personal definition and cannot understand why others pervert their meaning. The problems started with the founding fathers and their reasons for their participation in the American Revolution. The Federalists interpretation of *freedom* was the freedom to govern. The Jeffersonian definition seems to be inclined to describe it as freedom from government. That difference has carried down to this day. Both groups are loyal to their principles and have at times worked together to obtain the nebulous end goals. But each has had its own reward it was striving for, unaware of the difference of the other.

The elite merchants and gentleman farmers wanted to replace the authority of the English Crown in the lives of the people. The poorer class and self-sufficient people wanted to do away with the authority of the Crown over their lives. Each based their feelings on several generations of cause and effect relationship with the authority system that spoke for the Crown and how their group had been treated by that system. In the short term, the goals were the same: "Do away with the authority of the English Parliament and the King." Over the long term, the goals were vastly different.

The Federalist intellectuals were willing to accept the challenge of telling their fellow citizens what to do and how to live, for their betterment in life. They felt that God had ordained them to master plan their lives and the lives of others. Liberty and freedom were defined by formal and rigid principles developed by anointed and appointed leaders, in their concept. This group was primarily Norman, Anglo-Saxon and Puritan.

The Jeffersonian group thought life should be lived naturally without any excess of rules to encumber man's relationship with nature. Liberty and freedom were defined as fluid and informal concepts with leadership authorized by consensus elections of the citizens. This group was made up of the Celts of Scotland and Ireland.

Neither group were exclusively represented in any geographic area, but there seem to have been more Federalist feelings in the Northeast and more Jeffersonian feelings in the South.

The Federalist Party was not in favor of western expansion in the 1700's. They were happy with the boundaries of the Appalachian Mountains to contain the world they wanted to rule. If the west was to be opened to settlement—so be it. They would do their best to make the rules for it, as they saw fit. The adherents of Jeffersonian thought were the seedbed of the thought of "Manifest Destiny." To possess the whole continent was their implied goal. It was done with the fuzzy thought that by expanding into this great wilderness each man would have his own domain and could live on it as he pleased. Each man would be equal in this new world.

Neither system was well thought out or perfect in its concepts. That did not stop its believers from strongly and tenaciously identifying with the goals of "Liberty and Freedom" by their own definition. The supporters of the Crown in America were roundly berated by both groups.

After the Revolution, their different goals lead into the conflicts that again pitted them against England in the War of 1812. For the Northeastern citizen, it was over sovereignty; and for the new Western citizen, it was for expansion as well as personal sovereignty. Eastern historians say the War of 1812 was inconclusive and the events in the Northwest Territory were insignificant. The Federalist generals who organized western campaigns on tried European tactics were defeated by the Indians. The Jeffersonian-influenced militia and rangers, who used Indian guerrilla tactics, secured the territory.

Their efforts did settle the rights of territorial expansion for the western citizen. From a functional point of view, our northern boundary became the Great Lakes and not at the Ohio River. This expansion doubled the size of the U.S. Government land mass control. The boundary dispute was started by George Rogers Clark in the Revolutionary War time period and not clearly settled until the end of the War of 1812.

Squatters

When the Indiana Territory was first opened to settlement, most of the settlers were considered to be "squatters"—they occupied land that they did not have title to. There were several reasons for this. Some of the land was still considered to be Indian land. The official surveying of the land had not been made by the government, but the settlers were on the scene and laid claim to the most desirable of the unoccupied land with the intent of claiming title when it became available or selling their improvements to the legal owner when title was available.

Squatting had been practiced by the first European settlers in America. While vast land grants were given to the chosen by the European royalty, the machinery of actual settlement was cumbersome and questionable in the large uncharted lands of the east coast. In the opinion of the political, military, church and commercial interest, the settlers who squatted were considered as savages and unworthy subjects.

George Washington, who had vast holdings in the Ohio territory before the Revolutionary War, considered the squatters as "pitifully mean" and feared reprisals from them by the burning of his buildings if they were legally ousted. The Eastern papers described them as "poor miserable preemptors," "violators of all law" and "these ignorant and illiterate settlers." They were thought to be as dangerous to civilization as the Indians.

The people on the frontiers were divided in their opinions. One North Carolina Senator described them as ragged, dirty, brawling, brow-beating monsters, six-feet high, whose vocation is robbing, drinking, fighting and terrifying every peaceful man. Others thought of the squatters as the best part of the population of all the New States— inoffensive, harmless, and patient people who bore the vexations from government uncomplainingly. Daniel Webster thought the squatter possessed the character of a frontier man—hardy, adventurous and enterprising.

The squatter thought of himself as coming into the "Promised Land" like the ancient Jews came into Israel. He and his kin had prayed for land for generations and this was their chance to see their prayers answered. They came with few possessions and little education, but great hopes and expectations, and did not expect a life of ease but were determined to work hard to claim and improve the conquered land and harvest the fruits of their labor. To show appreciation of obtaining their long felt desires, words like "freedom," "liberty" and "pleasant" were used in many church and location names.

By moving west first, the early settlers served as a buffer between the more "civilized" east coast gentry who were moving west and the troublesome Indians. The early squatters did not pay for the land with cash, but many paid for it with their lives. From 1780 until 1815, nearly 2,000 settlers lost their scalps to the English Crown. Others died from cholera, milk sickness, yellow fever or malaria.

Squatters were known to have moved west three or four times before they reached their final homes. Most of the Midwestern families that have early ties to migration to this area before 1830 have squatters in their heritage. The squatter had the same attitude towards the unoccupied land as many have of a coin laying on the pavement in a parking lot: it is there, it is available and it is unclaimed.

Chapter 10
Why We Are Called Hoosiers

When traveling outside of Indiana and you meet a stranger and tell them you are from Indiana, one of the first things many of them want to know is "What is a Hoosier." The short answer is "a native born in Indiana and the true origin of the term is not known." The long answer is that there are a variety of origin stories.

The name HOOSIER is an evolved term. It started as "HUSSAR" in Indiana around 1818. This followed a period of terror and fear by the European settlers in the Indiana territory. Shortly before the War of 1812, the native Americans had been encouraged by the British in Canada to reclaim the land north of the Ohio River. In the areas that would become Jackson, Washington, Scott, Orange, Lawrence, Daviess and Knox counties, settlers were being killed in their cabins. Farmers had to take their rifle with them to the fields to prevent being killed by the natives. A bell tied around a horse's neck might be rung by the horse or by an Indian coaxing the settler into a deadly ambush as he tried to retrieve his horse, a most prized possession. A bird call in the woods might be a bird or an Indian coordinating an attack ambush on a settler.

Settler scalps were being bought by the British until 1813, usually with markings as to how the person had been killed: a man in battle, a farmer in his field, a settler burned at the stake, a woman in her cabin, or a unborn child torn from her mother's belly. Half of the new settlers fled the territory and returned to Kentucky. The terror continued after the war in the minds of the settlers. In 1817, a large winter encampment of Indians were living north of White River in the Sparksville area of Jackson County. It was rumored that just before their planned returned to their summer camps in the north, they were planning to massacre the settlers across the river from their camps. The settlers were terrified. Apparently they were encouraged to take bold actions against the cause of their fears. They were told stories of bold actions of Napoleon's Hussars in Europe.

Who Are Hussars?

"In battle, they were used in such light cavalry roles as harassing enemy skirmishers, overrunning artillery positions, and pursuing fleeing troops. Hussars were notoriously impetuous, and had a fearless resolve to obtain their goals regardlesss of the odds against them. Napoleon was quoted as stating that he would be surprised for a hussar to live beyond the age of 30 due to their tendency to become reckless in battle."

A famous military commander in Bonaparte's army who began his military career as a hussar was Marshal Michel Ney. After being employed as a clerk in an iron works, he joined the 5th Hussars in 1787. He rose through the ranks of the hussars in the wars of Belgium and the Rhineland (1794–1798), fighting against the forces of Austria and Prussia before receiving his marshal's baton in 1804, after the Emperor Napoleon's coronation. He was touted as the BRAVEST OF THE BRAVE in Napoleon's army. After the disastrous retreat from Russia, where most of the army perished due to the harsh weather, by Ney's leadership and command many of his men survived. Later he was given the French title of FIRST PRINCE OF MOSCOW for his heroics.

After the 1815 defeat of the French army at Waterloo and the Bourbons had returned to power, several of Napoleon's senior officers were tried and convicted of treason by the Bourbons. Ney was one and sentenced to a firing squad. Historians give one reason for the death of several senior officers was to stop the possibility of Napoleon again rising from exile to run the country.

After a fake firing squad death on December 7, 1815, Ney was smuggled out of France with another "executed" Napoleon military officer, Count Lehmanowsky, with the clandestine approval of Wellington. Lehmanowsky left the packet boat at Philadelphia while Ney went on to the ship's next stop, Charleston, South Carolina. He was shortly recognized by French Loyalists. Ney was afraid that the French Courts would find out about his existence and demand his extradition back to France. He fled to the wild and untamed frontier where he would not be known.

Legend has it that Field Marshall Ney was using the alias Peter Stuart Ney and living in the Washington County area from 1816 until 1818. Ney fled to the Old Northwest Territory that had been a French possession just 50 years before. One of his favorite haunts was a cave on Twin Creek near Campbellsburg, where he lived with a group of French fur trappers, living a trapper's lifestyle.

It is thought that as a military man of strong personality in a country that only three years before been subject to fierce Indian raids on the settlers cabins, he encouraged the population to be as strong, resilient and cunning to their hardships as the Hussars that had served under him in Europe. The locals were soon calling each other Hussars.

One of the first civic improvements in our southern Indiana area was the sponsorship of schools for the children. While life in the wilderness was hard for the new American settlers, the parents wanted to give their children a hope for the future. They thought that advantage was by giving them the ability to read, write and "do numbers." Many of the parents had come from eastern parts that had schools. They wanted the same advantage for their children.

The first schools in southern Indiana were in Washington County. Three of them were built in the 1809 to 1815 time period. The first school in the Lawrence County area was taught by an Irish monk, Alfred Landgon, at Leesville in 1814. The early school classes were held in the homes of the sponsoring parents. In 1818, Langdon moved west of Tunnelton and started classes at the James Conley farm, a short distance from the later location of the little tunnel on the B&O Railroad.

The first primitive school houses were one-room cabins about eighteen feet by twenty feet. After the building was raised, it was then notched down, shored and hewed. The roof was composed of poles and clapboard. The windows were made by cutting the upper half out of one log and the lower half of its neighbor above, and short sticks fastened in the opening at the proper intervals of space, upon which was pasted greased paper for window lights. The room was heated by a huge fireplace. It was made by cutting out one end of the building about twelve feet in width and six feet in height.

The seats of the school were strong and solid. They were made of small trees cut and split in half, and dressed on the top or split side and the bark removed from the under side. Holes were bored through the timber with a two-inch auger and pins put in for legs. The writing desks were equal in simplicity. Some holes were bored in the wall and strong pins driven in and some split puncheons boards, dressed down as smooth as they could be, laid on the pins—this was the writing desk.

Such was the school of the early days. No back to the seats, no drawers for books, no place for ink—in fact, none of the conveniences of later schools. Yet the children of that day were only too glad to get six weeks to two months of schooling. They made no complaint. Their text books were exceedingly meager. After a child was taught to read, they carried to school anything they could find in the home that would do to read. This might be a catechism, a history, a testament or Bible. Very few of the older pupils could afford arithmetic books, so they were taught mathematics without a book. Teachers gave rules and problems from a manuscript "sum book" which they themselves had made.

Schools had no blackboards and no maps, but occasionally a teacher owned a small globe which attracted a great deal of attention. Slate did not come into use until 1820, and lead pencils in 1835. The sum books were filled with homemade ink and pens made of goose quills. The ink was commonly made of the bark of the swamp maple, boiled down in an iron kettle to make the ink blacker. If the ink was allowed to freeze, it was spoiled.

The paper used in the school room was dark and rough. Its cost caused it to be used sparingly. It came in foolscap size (17 inches by 13.5 inches), without lines. For a writing book, each sheet was folded to make four leaves (8.5 inches by 6.75 inches), or eight pages. Enough of these were slipped within each other to form a book of desired thickness. Lastly, a cover of coarse brown paper was cut out to the size of the book and the whole thing sewed together. The children ruled the books themselves by means of a lead point, made from a bullet, which was kept tied to the ruler. The teacher always set the work to be copied at the top of each page, usually some moral precept like "Honesty is the best policy," etc. Many children soon became excellent scribes. From this background came most of the first store and bank clerks as well as many county government officials in southern Indiana.

The early schools of the area complained that there was little for their students to read after being taught their three "R's" of reading, 'riting and 'rithmetic. To help solve this shortage, the first book printed in Indiana was printed at Salem by Stout's Print Shop. The subject was the recent European military events of Napoleon. The book's title was *The Life of Napoleon Bonaparte* and was authored by "Citizen of the United States." The book described the adventures of Napoleon and played up the valor and bravery of the Hussars under his command. It is my contention that Marshal Ney was the "Citizen of the United States" credited with the authorship of the early Salem book, and that he popularized the term Hussar in that area.

Ney's traveling companion from France, Count Lehmanowsky, settled in Indiana in the 1830's and at one time he gave popular lectures about his European military experience under Napoleon. In his talks, he gave high praise to the "Hussars," a group of European soldiers renowned for their resource fullness and bravery.

A Salem native by the name of Short was helping build the Portland Canal at Louisville in the late 1820's. While working, he got into a fight with three fellow workmen and soundly flogged them. Remembering the Washington County stories about the Hussars and gloating over his victory, he cracked his fists and shouted, "Don't tackle me, I am a Hussar."

What Is a Hoosier?

Some of the Kentucky Colonels, in talking with their neighbors over a mint julep and a pipe bowl of tobacco about their neighbors north of the river in the knobs and valleys of Indiana, thought the reputation for Hussar cunning and bravery was wrong. Another term should be applied.

They were calling some of the dirty, illiterate and backward people living in the Appalachian Mountains "sons of Ireland" or "O'Eire's." They thought this better described the settlers north of the Ohio River. Some of the first generation Kentuckians also had a heavy English brogue. They usually started a word with a rough breathing "H" sound, so the term came to be known as "H' O'Eire" or "Hoosier."

Lyman Draper, in an 1843 letter to William Martin of Dixon Springs, Tennessee, mentioned a pronunciation problem that bears on this situation. Draper wrote:

"Haywood speaks of 'Heaton's Station'—in yours of 1st of Dec. you speak of the same. Now Gov. Campbell assures me it was 'Eaton's' not Heatons & Col. George Christian says so, too & adds that at all events the old man after whom it was named, was always known as 'Amos Eaton.' The particular mode of pronunciation as practiced in England with the rough breathing, would make 'Eaton' 'Heaton.' May not this have occurred in some way as this?"

Some Indiana historians who had researched the term Hoosier claim that the unusual "ier" or "sier" ending has always been difficult to explain. One possible source might be "O'Eire's" if an Englishman with a "rough breathing problem" tried to say "son of Ireland" (O'Eire) it would be heard as "h'O'Eire," a phonetic similarity to Hoosier.

The Kentucky neighbors were trying to insult the people north of the Ohio River by calling them Hoosiers. The settlers north of the river did not object to being called "Hoosiers" (sons of Ireland) since many of their families had come from Ireland.

In the early days of southern Indiana, travelers thought all the people north of the Ohio River were wild and unkept in comparison to the more "civilized" citizens of Kentucky. Early in the Indiana's existence, some visitors referred to the people they met by the derogatory term as applied to some of the lower class of Kentucky mountain citizens, that of being an "O'Eire," or a "Hoosier."

By their recent experiences on the frontier, the people north of the Ohio River cherished their independence and thought all people in Indiana were equal and expected to be treated as such. When an elite traveler encountered the Indiana locals and showed that he thought himself superior to them, the Hoosiers would slyly take advantage of him. If they could confuse, misguide or befuddle a stranger to their own advantage and to the hurt of the visitor, they felt justified in doing so since they were not being treated as an equal on their own soil. When the term "Hoosier" was applied by the frustrated foreigner, with a few choice and impolite adjectives, it was meant as a bold-faced insult. To the Hoosier in question, he took it as a badge of honor. The term was embraced by most of the early settlers and they started to call each other by this honored title, in jest and in seriousness.

Other stories about the origin of "Hoosier" include the following. A visitor would visit a remote cabin and knock on the door: the response was "Who's there?" Another familiar quote is "Who's your daddy?" A third story relates that after a knock-down, drag-out fight where the rules allowed for gouging out an eye, biting off a nose or chewing off an ear, one of the spectators found an ear on the floor asked "Who's ear is this?" Several other theories exist, albeit less known. Pugilistic Indiana rivermen became known as "hushers" because they were extremely successful in silencing their foes with fisticuffs. Construction workers responsible for the Louisville and Portland Canal in Louisville, Kentucky, were called "Hoosier's Men" after a supposed supervisor, Samuel Hoosier. "Hoosa" was a Native American word for corn: "Hoose" was an English term for a cattle disease: and "Hussar" was a term for light cavalry of Serbian origin used widely in Europe and Latin America during the 19th century. There is also the proclamation "Huzzah!" uttered after claiming victory in a fight.

The first known verbal usage of the term "Hussar/Hoosier" was in the early 1820's in the Campbellsburg area of Washington County. By the 1830s, the word "Hoosier" was widely used. In 1831, General John Tipton received a proposal from a businessman offering to name his boat the *Indiana Hoosier* if Tipton would give him business in the area. Whatever its origin, "Hoosier" first appeared in print in 1833, in a poem written by John Finley called "The Hoosier's Nest" describing the Hoosier citizens and the term stuck.

Chapter 11
Early Indiana Counties

The land mass that would later become Indiana was first identified as part of New France. In 1680, it was in a primarily undeveloped portion of the French New World territory. It was located in the far reaches of the Mississippi River system from the Gulf Coast control of Biloxi and New Orleans, and also in the ill-defined outback of the French control from Quebec and Montreal, Canada. Neither governmental area exerted very much control over this territory. It was an orphaned stepchild to both governmental units.

France ceded Canada in accordance with the 1763 treaty and the English took control of the area north of the Ohio River from Pittsburgh to the Mississippi River. They called this area the Northwest Territory. The American government took control of the Northwest Territory due to the peace treaty signed at the end of the Revolutionary War. Although the British had signed away the Northwest Territory rights, they did not remove their military influence in the area or support of the native tribes in that area until the end of the War of 1812 and Proctor's 1813 defeat in Canada.

As the land started to fill with European settlers, the Northwest Territory was broken into small political units by the United States government. On July 4, 1800, the the Indiana Territory was chartered and remained so until Indiana was admitted to the Union as the 19th state on December 11, 1816. Some Indiana counties had their origin in each of these political units.

KNOX
COUNTY

DEARBORN CO.

CLARK
COUNTY

HARRISON
COUNTY

**Indiana
1808**

(Indiana Population,
1800 Census: 2,632)

1808 map found in Lawrence County
Historical Society map collection that
gives then-current county boundaries.

(1) KNOX

ENTITY: Northwest Territory
ENTRY DATE: June 6, 1790
NAMED FOR: Henry Knox, U.S. Secretary of War

Henry Knox oversaw the nation's military activity in the Northwest Indian War. He was formally responsible for the nation's relationship with the Indian population in the territories it claimed, articulated a policy that established federal government supremacy over the states in relating to Indian nations, and called for treating Indian nations as sovereign. Knox's idealistic views on the subject were frustrated by ongoing illegal settlements and fraudulent land transfers involving Indian lands.

(2) CLARK

ENTITY: Indiana Territory, July 4,1800 to December 11, 1816
ENTRY DATE: February 3, 1801
NAMED FOR: General George Rogers Clark

George Rogers Clark was a military leader in the Revolutionary War in the Northwest Territory. He has often been hailed as the "Conqueror of the Old Northwest."

(3) DEARBORN

ENTITY: Indiana Territory
ENTRY DATE: March 7, 1803
NAMED FOR: Dr. Henry Dearborn, U.S. Secretary of War

Henry Dearborn was U.S. Secretary of War at the time the county was named.

(4) HARRISON

ENTITY: Indiana Territory
ENTRY DATE: December 1, 1808
NAMED FOR: Governor William Henry Harrison

Indiana Territorial Governor **William Henry Harrison** was the 1811 military leader at the Battle of Tippecanoe. He negotiated many Indiana land treaties with Indians.

(5) JEFFERSON

ENTITY: Indiana Territory
ENTRY DATE: November 23, 1810
NAMED FOR: Thomas Jefferson

Thomas Jefferson was principal author of the Declaration of Independence (1776) and the third President of the United States (1801–1809). He was an ardent proponent of democracy and embraced the principles of republicanism and the rights of the individual.

(6) WAYNE

ENTITY: Indiana Territory
ENTRY DATE: November 27, 1810
NAMED FOR: General "Mad" Anthony Wayne

Anthony Wayne was a Revolutionary War general and the first successful miltary campaigner to subdue western Indians in 1794. A direct result of his military efforts led to the 1795 Treaty of Greenville which granted large tracks of Northwest Territory lands for American settlers.

(7) **FRANKLIN**

ENTITY: Indiana Territory
ENTRY DATE: February 1, 1811
NAMED FOR: Benjamin Franklin
Benjamin Franklin earned the title of "The First American" for his early and indefatigable campaigning for colonial unity, first as an author and later spokesman in London for several colonies. As the first United States Ambassador to France, he exemplified the emerging American nation.

(8) **GIBSON**

ENTITY: Indiana Territory
ENTRY DATE: April 1, 1813
NAMED FOR: John Gibson, Secretary of Indiana Territory
John Gibson was the first appointed government official in Indiana Territory (1800); and in 1811, he became acting governor of Indiana Territory. Gibson moved the territorial capital from Vincennes to Corydon.

(9) **WARRICK**

ENTITY: Indiana Territory
ENTRY DATE: April 30, 1813
NAMED FOR:

Captain Jacob **Warrick**
Captain **Jacob Warrick** was mortally wounded at the Battle of Tippecanoe.

(10) **WASHINGTON**

ENTITY: Indiana Territory
ENTRY DATE: December 21, 1813
NAMED FOR: George Washington
Called the Father of the United States, **George Washington** presided over the convention that drafted the Continental Army during the American Revolutionary War, and was one of the Founding Fathers. He presided over the convention that drafted the current United States Constitution and during his lifetime was called the "father of his country." First President of the United States (1789–97).

KNOX
COUNTY

WAYNE CO.

UNORGANIZED

FRANKLIN
COUNTY

DEARBORN
COUNTY

JEFFERSON CO.

SWITZER-
LAND CO.

WASHINGTON
COUNTY

CLARK
CO.

GIBSON
COUNTY

HARRISON
CO.

PERRY
CO.

POSEY
CO.

WARRICK
CO.

**Indiana
1814**

1814 map found in Lawrence County Historical Society map collection that gives then-current county boundaries.

(Indiana Population, 1810 Census: 24,520)

(11) **SWITZERLAND**
ENTITY: Indiana Territory
ENTRY DATE: October 1, 1814
NAMED FOR: Settlers from Switzerland

(12) **PERRY**
ENTITY: Indiana Territory
ENTRY DATE: November 1, 1814
NAMED FOR: Oliver Hazard Perry
Oliver Hazard Perry earned the title "Hero of Lake Erie" for leading American forces in a decisive naval victory at the Battle of Lake Erie, receiving a Congressional Gold Medal and the thanks of Congress. His leadership materially aided the successful outcomes of all nine Lake Erie military campaign victories, and the fleet victory was a turning point in the battle for the west in the War of 1812. He is remembered for the words on his battle flag, "Don't Give Up the Ship."

(13) **POSEY**
ENTITY: Indiana Territory
ENTRY DATE: November 11, 1814
NAMED FOR: Thomas Posey,
    Indiana Governor
Thomas Posey (July 9, 1750–March 19, 1818) was an officer in the American Revolution, a general during peacetime, the third lieutenant governor of Kentucky, captain at Battle of Tippecanoe, governor of the Indiana Territory, and a Louisiana senator.

(14) **JACKSON**
ENTITY: Indiana Territory
ENTRY DATE: January 1, 1816
NAMED FOR:
    General Andrew Jackson
Andrew Jackson became a national hero for his actions in the War of 1812. He was described as "tough as old hickory" wood on the battlefield, and he acquired the nickname of "Old Hickory." In the Battle of New Orleans on January 8, 1815, Jackson's 5,000 soldiers won a decisive victory over 7,500 British.

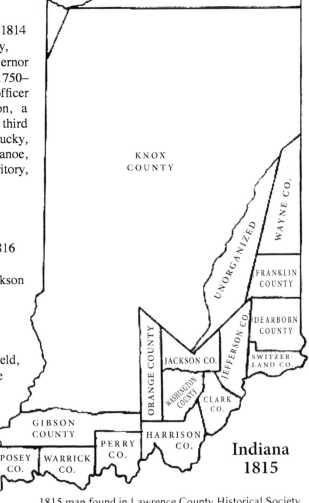

1815 map found in Lawrence County Historical Society map collection that gives then-current county boundaries.

(15) ORANGE
ENTITY: Indiana Territory, July 4, 1800 to December 11, 1816
ENTRY DATE: February 1, 1816
NAMED FOR: Orange County, North Carolina
(Orange County, North Carolina was named for the Dutch Protestant House of Orange.)

(16) PIKE
ENTITY: Indiana State, December 11, 1816 to present date
ENTRY DATE: December 21, 1816
NAMED FOR: Zebulon M. Pike, U.S. Western explorer
Zebulon Montgomery Pike (January 5, 1779–April 27, 1813) was an American brigadier general and explorer for whom Pike's Peak in Colorado is named. As a United States Army captain in 1806–1807, he led the Pike Expedition, sent out by President Thomas Jefferson, to explore and document the southern portion of the Louisiana Territory and to find the headwaters of the Red River, during which he recorded the discovery of what later was called Pike's Peak.

(17) JENNINGS
ENTITY: Indiana Territory
ENTRY DATE: December 27, 1816
NAMED FOR: Jonathan Jennings, Indiana Governor
Jonathan Jennings initially intended to practice law, but took jobs as an assistant at the federal land office at Vincennes and assistant to the clerk of the territorial legislature to support himself, and pursued interests in land speculation and politics.

(18) RIPLEY
ENTITY: Indiana State
ENTRY DATE: December 27, 1816
NAMED FOR: General Eleazen Wheelock Ripley
Eleazer Wheelock Ripley (April 15, 18721–March 2, 1839) was an American soldier and politician. He fought in the War of 1812, eventually rising to the rank of brigadier general, and later served as a U.S. Representative from Louisiana from 1835 until 1839.

(19) SULLIVAN
ENTITY: Indiana State
ENTRY DATE: December 30, 1816
NAMED FOR: Daniel Sullivan,
Revolutionary War General
Daniel Sullivan was killed by Native Americans while carrying a dispatch between Fort Vincennes and Louisville.

(20) DUBOIS
ENTITY: Indiana State
ENTRY DATE: December 20, 1817
NAMED FOR: Captain Toussaint Dubois
Toussaint Dubois (October 8, 1762–May 10, 1816) was a Montreal-born Frenchman and American soldier who joined with Lafayette to fight for American independence in the American Revolutionary War. As a captain, DuBois commanded the Company of Spies and Guides of the Indiana Militia at the 1811 Battle of Tippecanoe. He also

served as a Major in the War of 1812, commanding the Kentucky Mounted Spies. Dubois drowned in 1816 while crossing the Little Wabash River in Illinois, when he was returning from business in St. Louis, Missouri. He was buried in Vincennes.

(21) LAWRENCE
ENTITY: Indiana State
ENTRY DATE: January 7, 1818
NAMED FOR: James Lawrence, Naval Captain
James Lawrence (October 1, 1781–June 4, 1813) was an American naval officer. During the War of 1812, he commanded the U.S.S. *Chesapeake* in a single-ship action against H.M.S. *Shannon* commanded by Philip Broke. He is probably best known to-day for his last words, or dying command, "Don't give up the ship!"—which is still a popular naval battle cry, and which was invoked by Oliver Hazard Perry on his personal battle flag, adopted to commemorate his dead friend.

(22) VANDERBURGH
ENTITY: Indiana State
ENTRY DATE: January 7, 1818
NAMED FOR: Henry Vanderburgh, Indiana Territorial Judge
At the age of sixteen, **Henry Vanderburgh** was made a lieutenant in the 5th New York Regiment of the Continental Army in 1776. Later he was promoted to Captain of the 2nd New York Regiment. He served in the Continental Army until the end of the Revolutionary War. After the war, Vanderburgh relocated to the Indiana Territory. He was appointed a commissioner for the licensing of Merchants, Traders and Tavernkeepers for Knox County, Indiana, in 1792. Vanderburgh became Territorial Judge for the Indiana Territory, a position he held until his death in 1812. He was buried near Vincennes in Knox County.

(23) SPENCER
ENTITY: Indiana State
ENTRY DATE: January 10, 1818
NAMED FOR: Captain Spier Spencer
A native of Virginia, **Spier Spencer** moved to Kentucky with his parents. He married Elizabeth Polk, daughter of the noted Indian fighter Captain Charles Polk, in Bardstown, Nelson County, Kentucky. Spencer and his wife moved to Vincennes, Indiana. In 1809, Spencer was appointed by Governor William Henry Harrison as the first sheriff of Harrison County, Indiana. He moved his family to Corydon and served in that office until his death. Spencer and his wife ran The Green Leaf Tavern in their large log home on Oak Street. Governor William Henry Harrison and Lieutenant Governor Radcliff Boon stayed there when they came on official business, as did delegates to the 1816 Indiana Constitution Convention. When tensions grew high between the settlers and the Native Americans, Spencer organized the Harrison County Militia, known as the "Yellow Jackets" because of the color of their uniforms, for a campaign against them. The Battle of Tippecanoe on November 7, 1811, ended with Captain Spencer being seriously wounded during the battle. He was shot in the head and when he was being carried off the field, he was killed by a second shot. Spencer's horse and sword were brought back from the battle and were returned to his widow.

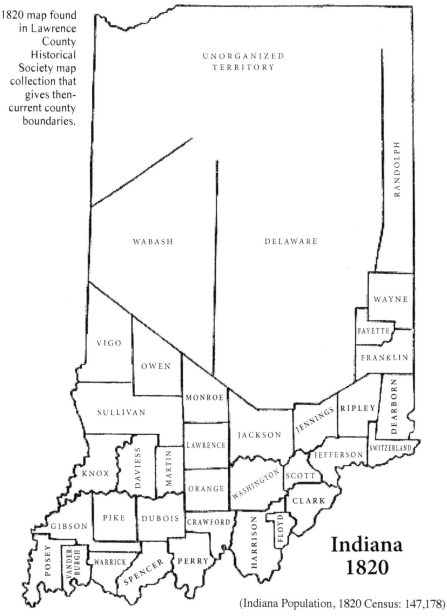

1820 map found in Lawrence County Historical Society map collection that gives then-current county boundaries.

UNORGANIZED TERRITORY

RANDOLPH

WABASH

DELAWARE

WAYNE

FAYETTE

FRANKLIN

VIGO

OWEN

DEARBORN

MONROE

SULLIVAN

JENNINGS

RIPLEY

JACKSON

LAWRENCE

DAVIESS

MARTIN

KNOX

ORANGE

WASHINGTON

JEFFERSON

SWITZERLAND

SCOTT

CLARK

PIKE

DUBOIS

CRAWFORD

GIBSON

HARRISON

FLOYD

POSEY

VANDER BURGH

WARRICK

SPENCER

PERRY

Indiana 1820

(Indiana Population, 1820 Census: 147,178)

(24) RANDOLPH
ENTITY: Indiana State
ENTRY DATE: January 10, 1818:
NAMED FOR: Randolph County, North Carolina
(Randolph County, North Carolina was named for the President of the Continental Congress.)

(25) MONROE
ENTITY: Indiana State
ENTRY DATE: January 14, 1818
NAMED FOR: President James Monroe

James Monroe (April 28, 1758–July 4, 1831) was the fifth President of the United States (1817–1825). Monroe was the last president who was a Founding Father of the United States, and the last president from the Virginia dynasty and the Republican Generation. Monroe was of the planter class and fought in the American Revolutionary War. After studying law under Thomas Jefferson from 1780 to 1783, he served as a delegate in the Continental Congress. As an anti-federalist delegate to the Virginia convention that considered ratification of the United States Constitution, Monroe opposed ratification, claiming it gave too much power to the central government. Monroe supported the founding of colonies in Africa for free African-Americans that would eventually form the nation of Liberia, whose capital, Monrovia, is named in his honor. In 1823, he announced the United States' opposition to any European intervention in the recently independent countries of the Americas with the Monroe Doctrine, which became a landmark in American foreign policy.

(26) VIGO
ENTITY: Indiana State
ENTRY DATE: January 21, 1818
NAMED FOR: Francis Vigo, Revolutionary War spy on the western front
Francis Vigo (born **Giuseppe Maria Francesco Vigo**, December 13, 1747–March 22, 1836) was an Italian-American who aided the American forces during the Revolutionary War. Born in Mondovi, Italy, he served with the Spanish Army in New Orleans. In 1772, he established a fur trading business in St. Louis. In 1783, Vigo moved to Vincennes and operated a fur trading business there. Vigo often aided American forces during the Revolutionary War, most famously as an informant to George Rogers Clark.

(27) FAYETTE
ENTITY: Indiana State
ENTRY DATE: January 29, 1818
NAMED FOR: Marquis de Lafayette
Marie-Joseph Paul Yves Roch Gilbert du Motier de Lafayette, Marquis de Lafayette (September 6, 1757–May 20, 1834), in the U.S. often known simply as Lafayette, was a French aristocrat and military officer who fought for the United States in the American Revolutionary War. A close friend of George Washington, Alexander Hamilton and Thomas Jefferson, he became convinced that the American cause in its revolutionary war was noble and travelled to the New World seeking glory in it. There he was made a major general, though initially the 19-year-old was not given troops to command. Wounded during the Battle of Brandywine, he still managed to organize an orderly retreat. He served with distinction in the Battle of Rhode Island. In the middle of the war, he returned home to lobby for an increase in French support. He again sailed to America in 1780, and was given senior positions in the Continental Army. In 1781, troops in Virginia under his command blocked forces led by Cornwallis until other American and French forces could position themselves for the decisive Siege of Yorktown. Lafayette was a key figure in the French Revolution of 1789, and the July Revolution of 1830.

(28) CRAWFORD
ENTITY: Indiana State
ENTRY DATE: January 29, 1818
NAMED FOR: Colonel William Crawford
William Crawford (September 2, 1732–June 11, 1782) was an American soldier and surveyor who worked as a western land agent for George Washington. Crawford fought

in the French and Indian War and the American Revolutionary War. Colonel William Crawford led the ill-fated expedition against the Sandusky Indians in June of 1782; he was defeated and, as a prisoner, he was tortured and burned at the stake by the Indians in retaliation for the Gnadenhutten massacre, a notorious incident near the end of the American Revolution in which Crawford did not participate.

(29) DAVIESS
ENTITY: Indiana State
ENTRY DATE: February 2, 1818
NAMED FOR: Major Joseph Hamilton Daveiss

Major **Joseph Daveiss** (March 4, 1774–November 7, 1811) was popularly known as "**Jo Daviess**." Although the correct spelling of his name appears to be "Daveiss," it is uniformly spelled "Daviess" in places named for him. Daveiss served as United States District Attorney for Kentucky. He has been described as a "Kentucky Federalist." In February and March 1806, he wrote President Thomas Jefferson several letters warning him of possible conspiratorial activities by Aaron Burr. Daveiss's July 14 letter to Jefferson stated flatly that Burr planned to provoke a rebellion in Spanish-held parts of the West in order to join them to areas in the Southwest to form an independent nation under his rule. Jefferson dismissed Daveiss's accusations against Burr, a Democratic-Republican, as politically motivated. In 1806, Daveiss brought treason charges against Burr in Kentucky. The charges were, however, dismissed thanks to the help of Burr's attorney, Henry Clay.

In 1811, Daveiss volunteered to serve in the Indiana Militia, answering Governor Harrison's call for troops to march against Tecumseh's village at Prophetstown. He was placed in command of two companies of dragoons and all the cavalry in Harrison's army. On the night of November 6, 1811, Harrison's army made camp near Prophetstown. Major Daveiss' dragoons occupied a position in the rear of the left flank. The dragoons were instructed to fight dismounted, with pistols, as a reserve in the event of a night attack. When the Indians attacked early the next morning, Major Daveiss advanced toward the heaviest fire with a small detachment. He was driven back and mortally wounded in the process. He died soon after. At the time of the Battle of Tippecanoe, Daveiss was serving as the eighth Grand Master of Masons of the Grand Lodge of Kentucky. He was a member of Lexington Lodge #1.

(30) OWEN
ENTITY: Indiana State
ENTRY DATE: December 21, 1818
NAMED FOR: Colonel Abraham Owen

Abraham Owen or **Abram Owen** (1769–1811) was born in Prince Edward County, Virginia, in 1769. He moved to Kentucky in 1785. Owen served in the wars with the Indians under generals James Wilkinson and Arthur St. Clair in 1791, and served with Colonel John Hardin. Owen was surveyor of Shelby County, Kentucky, in 1796. He was in the Kentucky Legislature in 1798, and a member of the State constitutional convention the next year. Owen served as a colonel and as aide-de-camp to William Henry Harrison at the Battle of Tippecanoe, where he was killed in 1811.

(31) FLOYD
ENTITY: Indiana State
ENTRY DATE: January 2, 1819
NAMED FOR: Colonel John Floyd (or) Davis Floyd
Colonel Floyd was an adjutant at the Battle of Tippecanoe.

Colonel **James John Floyd** (1750–April 10, 1783), better known as **John Floyd**, was a pioneer around the Louisville, Kentucky, area where he worked as a surveyor for land development and as a military figure. Floyd was an early settler of St. Matthews, Kentucky, and helped lay out Louisville. In Kentucky, he served as a Colonel of the Kentucky Militia in which he participated in raids with George Rogers Clark, and later became one of the first judges of Kentucky. In September 1776, Floyd left Boonesborough and returned to Virginia. Floyd traveled to Williamsburg and signed on to a privateering syndicate and agreed to serve on board the Massachusetts schooner *Phoenix*. Instructions given to *Phoenix* captain Joseph Cunningham of Boston indicated the schooner was to sail from Yorktown, Virginia, to the West Indies for a three-month voyage. Floyd sailed out of Chesapeake Bay in early January of 1777. The *Phoenix* successfully arrived back in Boston in early April 1777, but without Floyd, who had been captured and transported to Forton Prison near Portsmouth, England. In late October of 1777, Floyd escaped from Forton and found his way to Paris. On October 30, 1777, Floyd received assistance in Paris from Benjamin Franklin and others who agreed to advance him funds to return to Virginia.

Davis Floyd (1776–December 13, 1834) was an Indiana Jeffersonian Republican politician who was convicted of aiding American Vice President Aaron Burr in the Burr Conspracy. Floyd was not convicted of treason, however, and returned to public life after spending several years working to redeem his reputation.

(32) DELAWARE
ENTITY: Indiana State
ENTRY DATE: January 1, 1820
Soon dissolved due to lack of population. Reorganized January 26, 1827.

(33) SCOTT
ENTITY: Indiana State
ENTRY DATE: January 12, 1820
NAMED FOR: Charles Scott, Kentucky Governor
Charles Scott visited the western frontier in 1785 and began to make preparations for a permanent relocation. He resettled near present-day Versailles, Kentucky, in 1787. Confronted by the dangers of Indian raids, Scott raised a company of volunteers in 1790 and joined Josiah Harmar for an expedition against the Indians. After Harmar's defeat, President Washington ordered Arthur St. Clair to prepare for an invasion of Indian lands in the Northwest Territory. In the meantime, Scott, by now holding the rank of brigadier general in the Virginia Militia, was ordered to conduct a series of preliminary raids. In July 1791, he led the most notable and successful of these raids against the village of Ouiatenon. St. Clair's main invasion, conducted later that year, was a failure. Scott's decision to appoint William Henry Harrison as brevet major general in the Kentucky Militia, although probably in violation of the state constitution as Harrison was not a resident of the state, was nonetheless praised by the state's citizens.

(34) MARTIN
ENTITY: Indiana State
ENTRY DATE: January 17, 1820
NAMED FOR: Major John T. Martin of Newport, Kentucky
Major **John T. Martin** was a hero of the War of 1812.

(35) WABASH
ENTITY: Indiana State
ENTRY DATE: January 20, 1820
Soon dissolved due to lack of population. Reorganized January 30, 1833.

Index

95